Six Ways to Pray From Six Great Saints

Six Ways to Pray From Six Great Saints

Gloria Hutchinson

Nihil Obstat:
   Rev. Greg Tajchman, O.F.M.
   Rev. John J. Jennings

Imprimi Potest:
   Rev. Jeremy Harrington, O.F.M.
   Provincial

Imprimatur:
   + Daniel E. Pilarczyk, V.G.
   Archdiocese of Cincinnati
   November 2, 1981

Cover, book design and illustrations by Julie Lonneman.

SBN 0-86716-007-1

RL-463

To
those who would learn
prayer
from our ancestor-saints.

Contents

Introduction

After dallying with the idea for several years, a young woman finally decided to learn the skills of mountain-climbing. She had climbed only a few easy peaks; but she had often talked, while sitting at a friend's kitchen table or lying on the beach, of tackling Mount McKinley, a feat her great-grandfather had accomplished in his youth. Now she was determined to act on her neglected intentions.

She read books about the basics of climbing. She sought out climbers to question, workshops to attend. Oddly enough, she ignored her great-grandfather's journal—even though his expertise in mountaineering had always been a source of family pride.

Asked why she did not look to him for guidance, the young woman seemed surprised. "I guess I thought he'd be kind of out-of-date. A little archaic, you know? Besides, what would an old pro like him have to say to a beginner like me?"

If this poor parable were applied to the art of prayer, how many of us could see ourselves in this near-sighted young woman?

Although we have among our own ancestors great masters of prayer, we seldom approach them for advice. We are heirs who forget to claim our inheritance. The legacy of the saints sits undusted on the shelf while we seek help from contemporary gurus who speak our language.

But who knows the language of prayer better than the saints? Despite their distance from us in time and culture, despite the chasm of perfection their biographers have created between them and us, the saints have not lost their effectiveness as teachers of prayer.

This book attempts to reach across the gulf and tap the prayer-experience of six holy men and women:

Francis of Assisi, whom we love to lionize but rarely consult in matters of prayer;

Clare of Assisi, as distant and perfect as the full moon;
Ignatius of Loyola, elite companion of Jesuits and 30-day
   retreatants;
Therese of Lisieux, whose Victorian language seems as
   prettified as a ruffled pinafore;
Teresa of Avila, the mystic roaming her interior castle;
John of the Cross, the poetic genius shrouded in a cloud of
   contemplation.

All of them were once beginners; none of them has forgotten how to initiate others who think of themselves as amateurs. They can and will speak to us of how to pray—if we have the patience and the good old-fashioned respect to listen.

What follows is not a comprehensive study of how these six saints prayed or a full disclosure of all they have to teach us. It is only an apple taken from a laden bough, polished and held out in the hope that a few bites will entice the reader back to the tree.

To avoid the pitfall of thinking or talking about prayer instead of praying, the heart of this book is meditations which reflect the counsel of each saint. Each chapter follows the same pattern:

Getting to know the saint and his or her style of prayer;
Praying both with the saint and on one's own;
Exploring further.

The "getting-to-know" section begins with a brief *life-sketch* to provide a nodding acquaintance with the saint about to be consulted. Moving in a little closer, a *portrait* is then drawn which, like a faded photograph in the family album, gives a few clues about the personality and character of the ancestor-saint. Then the focus narrows to the saint's *prayer-life*, providing the context for the lesson in prayer.

This prayer lesson/experience is the place to center down and let the saint-tutor teach prayer. It begins by suggesting one way the reader might make the saint's prayer his or her own. This *approach* offers a single prayer-form as a possible vehicle. An *invocation*, an appeal to the saint-tutor for assistance, sets the stage for prayer and makes the transition from talking about prayer to praying.

A *meditation/reflection* set in the saint's own time and space is followed by a complementary *meditation/reflection* which returns the reader to his or her own life. The chapters on Francis, Clare and Therese provide two such pairs of meditations; other chapters offer one.

These meditations are to be prayed, not just read. They require an active use of the imagination, the mind and the will. The goal in each case is to seek God via a path illumined by one of his saints. To follow in their footsteps, the reader may have to wade deep into unfamiliar waters, leaving preconceptions and prejudices about prayer in a bundle on the shore.

Further explorations into the type of prayer just practiced in company with a saint are suggested at the end of each chapter. These include a brief bibliography for those who would like more intimate acquaintance with their tutors.

If the meditations in this book prove enjoyable or enlightening, that is a fringe benefit—nice to have but not necessary to our survival as prayerful persons. We pray to be present in loving attention to our God. We meditate in the hope of deepening our receptivity to the love with which he would lure us to him, as he captured the hearts of the saints who have gone before us.

To this end we come to sit, Mary-like, at the feet of the masters. Each of them mirrors Christ in a singular way; all were taught by the same—the ultimate—teacher of prayer:

> The Spirit too helps us in our weakness, for we do not know how to pray as we ought; but the Spirit himself makes intercession for us with groanings that cannot be expressed in speech. He who searches hearts knows what the Spirit means, for the Spirit intercedes for the saints as God himself wills.
>
> (Rom 8:26-27)

Come, Spirit Lord, teach us to pray.

FRANCIS
OF ASSISI
1182-1226

The Wounded Herald

Getting to Know Francis

Life-Sketch   Francis was the 13th century's Mother Teresa of Calcutta.
Known, loved, honored, imitated, called a saint to his face
(much to his shame), Francesco Bernadone was *Il Poverello,* the
"Little Poor Man" who gave poverty a good name. But all that
came after his conversion.

Before he began listening to Christ, Francesco was a
swinger, a spender, a charmer who gadded about Assisi chasing
amusement's kite-tail. The son of a middle-class cloth merchant,
he reveled in fine wardrobes, practical jokes and parties where he
spared himself few pleasures. His dreams of chivalrous heroism
were lanced by the Perugians, who imprisoned him for a year
during one of several wars with Assisi.

For the first time in his life, the irrepressible Francis had to
sit still and take stock of himself. Prison freed him from the
constant stimulation of socializing and puffing up his popularity.
He began to have symbolic religious dreams and brief mystical
experiences. Upon his release, he attempted to revive his old
merrymaking ways but physical illness, guilt and the aftertaste of
futility haunted him.

Francis wandered for months, a nomad in the desert of
spiritual awareness. Then he stumbled into the ruins of San
Damiano, a chapel dedicated to a wonder-working physician-
saint. From the life-sized Byzantine crucifix that today hangs in the
Basilica of St. Clare in Assisi, Jesus spoke to Francis: "Go and
repair my church which, as you see, is falling into ruin."

Responding with a literalness that would always
characterize his spirituality, Francis threw himself into the task at
hand. Noah could not have been a more fervent builder. The
Little Poor Man, divested of his wardrobe, his parents and his
admiring friends, rushed from one construction site to another,
repairing churches with the zeal of an ambitious pastor.

The Lord let Francis run his high-speed convert's course for
a while before revealing to the Poverello that the task had broader

dimensions. The medieval Catholic Church itself, rife with corruption and immorality, was in need of rehabilitation. Francis, by his gospel life of poverty, purity and charity, would erect a scaffolding for the endangered edifice. The thousands who would follow him in the Friars Minor, the Poor Clares and the Third Order were Francis' ultimate answer to the request Jesus made at San Damiano.

Portrait To his contemporaries, Francis was an inspired oddball in beggar's garb. Thomas of Celano, his biographer, describes him as a black-eyed, bearded, short-legged, thin-lipped figure that "bore the very minimum of flesh."

Despite his ragtag appearance, Francis had an energy that captivated and compelled. His preaching moved man and bird and beast. They sensed in Francis the fusion of message and messenger. In him, the gospel was undiluted by comfort or wealth, security or prestige, theologizing or temporizing. When Francis set out to imitate Christ, he took an unselective approach. He didn't decide to emulate the Master's humility or his compassion or his courage. He embraced the whole Christ, desiring to be like him in every way.

Francis fasted and prayed for 40 days in the wild reaches of Mount La Verna in the Italian Apennines. From the time of his conversion he was drawn to the hermit's solitary life with God. But the Lord made his will known through the prayerful counsel of Sister Clare and Brother Sylvester: "He wants you to go about the world preaching, because God did not call you for yourself alone but also for the salvation of others."

Francis obeyed, fueling his missionary treks with brief retreats and night-long vigils. Towards the end of his life, he felt called to contemplation of the Passion. The intensity of his prayer on La Verna drew down a flaming seraph that wounded him with the stigmata, stamping him with the identity he cherished.

Afterwards, Francis felt half-alien. He longed for Sister Death to take him home. But death delayed and the Little Poor

Man went on for two more years, praising and preaching, suffering himself and healing others.

While he waited, he sang. "The Canticle of Brother Sun" poured out of him like full-bodied wine from a sturdy barrel. Neither his wounds nor his near-blindness prevented Francis from carrying on as Christ's minstrel, the Italian herald of the Good News. His poetry, to borrow a phrase from Gerard Manley Hopkins, was "charged with the grandeur of God." In "The Canticle of Brother Sun," he sang until the Lord himself could no longer resist:

> Most high, all-powerful, all good, Lord!
>   All praise is yours, all glory, all honor
>   And all blessing.
> To you, alone, Most High, do they belong.
>   No mortal lips are worthy
>   To pronounce your name.
> All praise be yours, my Lord, through all that you have made,
>   And first my lord Brother Sun,
>   Who brings the day; and light you give to us through him.
> How beautiful is he, how radiant in all his splendor!
>   Of you, Most High, he bears the likeness.
> All praise be yours, my Lord, through Sister Moon and Stars;
>   In the heavens you have made them, bright
>   And precious and fair.
> All praise be yours, my Lord, through Brothers Wind and Air,
>   And fair and stormy, all the weather's moods,
>   By which you cherish all that you have made.
> All praise be yours, my Lord, through Sister Water,
>   So useful, lowly, precious and pure.
> All praise be yours, my Lord, through Brother Fire,
>   Through whom you brighten up the night.
>   How beautiful is he, how gay! Full of power and strength.
> All praise be yours, my Lord, through Sister Earth, our mother,
>   Who feeds us in her sovereignty and produces
>   Various fruits with colored flowers and herbs.
> All praise be yours, my Lord, through those who grant pardon
>   For love of you; through those who endure
>   Sickness and trial.
> Happy those who endure in peace,
>   By you, Most High, they will be crowned.

All praise be yours, my Lord, through Sister Death,
From whose embrace no mortal can escape....

Francis was never satisfied with half-measures. He loved with a rashness that made many holy souls and humanitarians look like emotional paupers. Not content to father his followers with counsel and protection, he also mothered them by domestic serving and nursing. He mirrored Christ's androgyny, joining tenderness to strength, discipline to compassion, Martha to Mary.

His poverty was an armor shielding him from the entanglements of materialism and vanity. Worry cannot compromise a man who welcomes homelessness and hunger. Francis was free beyond the dreams of those who equate freedom with self-sufficiency or self-indulgence.

Although he never honored suffering for its own sake, he neither hid from pain nor muffled it with loud complaint. Francis never forgot that Christ first spoke to him from the cross. Suffering was the medium by which the image of Jesus was transferred to Francis. It provoked praise, not condemnation.

Prayer was Francis' native tongue. He spoke it with heart, intellect and body. When he prayed, he summoned his entire self into focus: memory, will, imagination, tired limbs, aching back, eyes seeking the stimulation of color and movement. He fastened on the presence of God and did not let go. His friars would no more interrupt him at prayer than wrest a steak from a hungry beggar. Neither boredom nor stupor would interfere with his night-long concentration on five syllables: "My God and my all!"

When he was alone in the woods, the Poverello's prayer became an ad-libbed song with imagined violin music. In a penitential season, praying was fasting and letting the Passion sink into his bones. In a time of decision, prayer for Francis was opening the Scriptures and allowing the Word to take hold of him, turn him around, set him on his ear:

Go and sell what you have.... (Mk 10:21)

Proclaim the kingdom of God. (Lk 9:60)

Whoever wishes to be my follower must deny his very self.... (Lk 9:23)

His biographer, St. Bonaventure, says of Francis: "Prayer was his sure refuge in everything he did; he never relied on his own efforts, but put his trust in God's loving providence and cast the burden of his cares on him in insistent prayer."

Bonaventure chose his adjective well. Like the widow who importuned the judge (see Lk 18:1-8), Francis prayed *insistently*. His requests were shored up by humility and affection. He believed he was the apple of his Father's eye; he was certain that a persistent son would not be denied.

Francis, however, did not make petition his primary form of prayer. His *Rule of 1221* affirms to his followers that priority must be given to praise and thanksgiving. "We should wish for nothing else and have no other desire; we should find no pleasure or delight in anything except our Creator, Redeemer and Savior..." (Ch. 23). If this single-mindedness seems unnatural, we can remind ourselves that Francis found God in all creation: in a leper's face, a lark's song, a lamb's docility. He loved the Lord he saw in Sister Clare and Brother Leo, the closest companions of his heart.

The Poverello was the personification of St. Paul's advice, "Dedicate yourselves to thankfulness" (Col 3:15). When he was turned away from shelter in a storm, abused and insulted, given scraps for dinner or a stone for a pillow, he responded with gratitude—not because he was demented enough to enjoy deprivation but because he appreciated the opportunity to experience the bodily sufferings of Christ. Francis found the Lord in all the circumstances of his life.

Prayer for him was never limited to prescribed times or places or rites. He made of his life a "holy leisure," an openness to God's presence whenever, wherever, however the Spirit came to him. Sometimes he turned *to* prayer; other times, he turned *into* prayer. One observer said of him, "He seemed not so much a man praying as prayer itself made man."

His encounters with God in secret propelled him from town to town, bearing the gospel like a victory banner. He advised his brothers that a preacher must be fired up by private prayer before he attempts to utter one word of a sermon: "He must first grow hot within before he speaks words that are in themselves cold."

Francis preached more by example than by eloquence. Once, when the Poor Ladies of San Damiano (Poor Clares) insisted on hearing a sermon from their beloved founder, he stood in front of them, raised his eyes in prayer and then asked that a bucket of ashes be brought to him. He circled himself with ashes and showered the remainder over his head. In silence, he remained standing before the shocked sisters. Finally, he recited Psalm 51 ("Have mercy on me, O God...") and left without further comment. The Little Poor Man understood the power of symbolism and the power of silence in leading others to prayer.

Letting Francis Teach Us

Approach   Few of us can imitate Francis' approach to prayer as
literally as he interpreted the Gospels. His prayer was a
reflection of his singular identity as the stigmatized herald of the
great King. It grew out of the radical circumstances of his life,
that holy leisure that brooked no interference from habitual
employment, property ownership or family obligations.

We can, however, distill what is characteristic about
Francis' prayer—his vibrant sense of praise and his devotion to
the Passion of Jesus—and consider how his experience can
nourish our own prayer. Our intention is not to copy the
Poverello (as did Friar Giovanni the Simple who mimicked
Francis' every sneeze and gesture in the hope of gaining
holiness), but to reflect on how the nature of his relationship
with God can influence us.

Consideration   Can Francis lead us to a fuller expression of praise in our
life—particularly when we are weakened, restricted or
discouraged?

Are we willing to give praise when we are wounded by
illness, imprisonment, addiction, loneliness, rejection,
failure?

Invocation   Francis,
little father in faith,
let me see you in solitary prayer.
Your brothers were never allowed to watch you
because you feared the consequences of their admiration.
You remembered the words of Jesus:

> When you are praying, do not behave like the
> hypocrites who love to stand and pray in synagogues
> or on street corners in order to be noticed. I give
> you my word, they are already repaid. (Mt 6:5)

Relent now.
Allow me to be there on La Verna's ledge,
sensing the depth of your sorrow
and the impact of Christ's response.
Banish my fear of any prayer powerful enough
to convert suffering into rapture.
You who were nearly blind, open my eyes
that I might see God-in-all
and sing my own canticle to his glory.

Praying With Francis:
La Verna

Meditation On the ragged peak of Mount La Verna, the wind shrieks
like a tormented schizophrenic in solitary confinement.
The September night is harsh at 3,000 feet, and the stars give
cold comfort. You have come here, Francis, to be alone, to
repent, to face the prospect of death. The desolation of this place
is fitting. Here life is reduced to essentials: no comforts, no
diversions, no inviting scenery, no calls to service. Just you and
the stern mountain.

Leo and the others have built you a rough hut on this
precipice and retired into the woods, separated from you by a
chasm. Their presence would be a consolation. But you will not
be turned aside from prayer. You clench your teeth against the
cold and withdraw further into your dark abode. The aching of
your bones and muscles threatens your resolve.

Instinctively, you protect yourself with prayer: "Jesus is
my only light!"

The light is all you need. Consolation and hope are
luxuries which you, who would know Christ crucified, cannot
afford. Crucial questions haunt the stillness. "Who are you, my
dearest Lord? And who am I, a miserable worm and useless
servant?" You fear the answers, yet you long to hear them.

13

Jesus has already obliged you by speaking through your randomly opened book of the Gospels. Three times the pages fell open to the Passion, and trepidation yawned before you as clearly as the chasm at your doorstep. To be like him in his suffering and torment before death comes! There it is: the final earthly fulfillment, the desired likeness—what you have wanted and not wanted. You would be a fool if you did not fear the meaning of that open book:

> When noon came, darkness fell on the whole countryside and lasted until midafternoon. At that time Jesus cried in a loud voice, *"Eloi, Eloi, lama sabachthani?"* which means, "My God, my God, why have you forsaken me?" (Mk 15:33-34)

It is the feast of the Exaltation of the Holy Cross. You know your prayer will be answered. "Lord, be merciful to me." Raising your arms to the stars, you await his coming, so familiar and incomprehensible. Dawn will soon soften the mountain's face and Leo will be there with bread and water. Life will go on, comforting you with the security of daily routine.

Perhaps the book was not to be taken literally. Perhaps you have misunderstood. The sound of your heart, pumping with anticipation, blocks these easy exits. "Lord, be merciful to me!"

A sudden light sets you off balance. Its brilliance blinds and disorients you. Shielding your eyes, you see the light converging on a fiery figure, a fantastic life-sized figure ablaze with flames that do not devour. A stunning seraph with incandescent wings—two raised heavenward, two stretched outward as for flight, two folded over the torso—hovers over you, defying your imagination and stopping thought as swiftly as a stroke.

You can do nothing. Only your eyes remember their appointed role. They note the five glowing wounds which mark the seraph's hands, feet, side. Your mind remains inert, unable to respond.

The seraph's face becomes visible, startling you with its exquisite sorrow and beauty. You strain for speech. Suddenly five beams of light shoot from the wounds. They find their targets in your flesh. With a loud voice that seems to come from someone else, you shout, "Jesus!" The blazing figure closes in on you, impresses itself on you, is swallowed up within you.

You fall forward on your face in the damp moss. Rapture holds you like a helpless child on her lap. Soon pain will make its presence known. But for now you are aware only of joy burning like a vigil light in the center of your being. For this brief span your search, your struggle, your questions are over. Christ has come to you. And you have become Christ.

Reflection   Francis could say with St. Paul, "I bear the brand marks of the Lord Jesus in my body" (Eph 6:17). Because he interpreted the Gospels so literally, it was fitting that his identification with the Crucified should take the explicit form of the stigmata. Figurative wounds would not have been enough for the saint who bore the image of Jesus so faithfully in his life-style, his ministry, his prayer.

> Do I, like Francis, pray with hope and authentic expectation?

> Does my life, in any way, reflect the wounded Christ?

> How often have I meditated on the Passion of Jesus and on what his suffering means to me?

Praying Like Francis: La Verna in My Life

Meditation   Jesus, I want, like Francis, to focus on your Passion and assimilate it into my life. I will prepare myself for this encounter by fasting and by setting myself apart from the company of others. I will seek no comfort beyond the belief that my prayer is, in some undefinable sense, a consolation to you.

I place myself on La Verna, a setting of isolation and physical extremity. For me, the mountain may be a barren room with a crucifix, a hospital bed, an empty chapel. If I am tired or my head aches, if I am ill or injured, weak or disheartened, I will make no complaint. I will accept and affirm whatever frailty I now experience as a bond between us.

Help me, Lord. This goes against the grain. Let your ways be my ways. I will remember Gethsemani, the Via Dolorosa, Calvary. And I will not turn away, pretending that these historic places exert no influence on the way I live my life.

Who are you, Lord? And who am I?

You are Jesus:

> the just one, the merciful, the ever-forgiving,
> sinned against but never sinning,
> the lasting Truth, the only Way,
> the bountiful host, the beloved brother,
> the servant-king, the bearer of pain,
> Redeemer and Lord.

And I am N._____,

> your sometimes unprofitable servant,
> a bridesmaid with a burned-out lamp,
> a grain of wheat afraid to be ground,
> a prodigal motivated by pride,
> a denying Peter, a reluctant Cyrenean,
> a distant observer at Calvary,
> a doubting Thomas.

Jesus, let me see your wounds close up so they sear my memory.

I see rejection, Jesus...

...By the Pharisees who did their best to discredit and despise you: "This man can expel demons only with the help of Beelzebul, the prince of demons" (Mt 12:24).

...By your friends and neighbors who did their best to bury you with righteous indignation because a prophet is without honor in his native place: "They rose up and expelled him from the town, leading him up to the brow of the hill on which it was built and intending to hurl him over the edge" (Lk 4:29-30).

...By the Chosen People, your Father's favorites, the wayward chicks that refused to be gathered under your maternal wings. From the hill above Jerusalem you wept and cried out to them: "If only you had known the path to peace this day; but you have completely lost it from view!" (Lk 19:42)

I see betrayal, Jesus...

...By your headstrong friend Peter, your wavering right arm, your blustering shepherd who refused to accept the prophecy that the wolves would slay the Lamb. You scolded him, "Get out of my sight, you satan! You are trying to make me trip and fall. You are not judging by God's standards but by man's" (Mt 16:23). And again when Peter forgot that he was your Rock and became a shiftless pebble swept ashore in a sea of apprehension: "I do not even know the man!" (Mt 26:74).

...By Judas, your zealous friend, who ate at your table and turned on you with a burning kiss. "Friend, do what you are here for!" (Mt 26:50).

I see hatred and humiliation, Jesus...

...Hurled at you by the high priest and the Sanhedrin: "Some of them began to spit on him. They blindfolded him and hit him, saying, 'Play the prophet!'" (Mk 14:65).

...By the enraged and orchestrated crowd: "Crucify him!" (Mk 15:13).

...By the professional soldiers who honed their cruelty on the whetstone of your humility: "Continually striking Jesus on the head with a reed and spitting at him, they genuflected before him and pretended to pay him homage" (Mk 15:19).

I see agony, Jesus...

...Drawn out, stretched beyond endurance, ravaging the body and testing the spirit in the night garden when the vise of dread and loneliness gripped and bled you: "My heart is nearly broken with sorrow" (Mt 26:38).

...Scourged, thorn-crowned, thirsting, jeered at and prodded, laden with a crossbeam like a pack animal, you drag your abused body along the Via Dolorosa. The air is thick with

17

curses and depraved laughter. The smell of slaughtered lambs hangs over the marketplace.

The crude nails rip through you like bolts of vengeful lightning and the weight of your body becomes the weight of the world, upheld only by your obedient arms. A thirst keener than the desert's plagues you. Agony wrenches an unwilling cry: *"Eloi, Eloi, lama sabachthani?"* (Mk 15:34).

Again a terrible cry, compressing all human agony into one voice of ultimate suffering: "Father, into your hands I commend my spirit" (Lk 23:46).

Jesus, here I am, ready to be wounded, to accept whatever suffering enters my life out of love for you. I recognize that crucifixion has as much to do with me as it does with you. How can I call myself by your name while holding your Passion at arm's length? Like Francis, I want to suffer knowingly, gladly, fully aware of the resemblance your love imprints on me.

Reflection   Am I afraid, Jesus, that you might ask me, in ways I would not choose, to share your agony?

What consolation do you hold out to me in my unwillingness to approach the cross?

What words of yours come to me when I reflect on my feelings about being wounded?

Praying With Francis: San Damiano

Meditation   Francis, I see you now in the garden at San Damiano. The brothers have built a wattle hut where you can recuperate from your illness and be cared for by Sister Clare. The cypress trees shade you and the silvery olive branches enchant you with their symbolism. While the sun shines, your fading sight feasts on the green patterns of the valley below.

Now and then Brother Leo comes to inquire about your health. You assure him that all is well; there is nothing more he can do. When night robs you of colors and voices, you begin to pray in earnest. Ever since Christ spoke to you in this sacred place, you have made the hours of darkness a time of intense prayer.

With the psalmist, you can say:

> Though you test my heart, searching it in the night,
>   though you try me with fire, you shall find no malice in me.
>   (Ps 17:3)

> By day the LORD bestows his grace,
>   and at night I have his song,
>   a prayer to my living God. (Ps 42:9)

But tonight and for the past several nights your prayer has been hindered by the creatures who wander in from the garden and make the hut their own. You have not been able to call these scampering field mice and contentious rats your brothers. Unable to see them, you are intermittently shocked and repulsed as their bodies fall heavily on your face or chest.

Pain is no stranger to you. And you are not one to sidestep discomfort. But this constant irritation, this obstacle to prayer, is too much. The rats are defiling your fellowship with the night and throttling the poetic impulses of your nature.

Offended beyond patience, you beg the Lord to banish them. It seems little enough to ask. The answer, however, heard within, is that one who is going to receive the treasure of eternal salvation should not complain about ephemeral things. Heartened by the promise, blooming like a rose on the thorny branch of denial, you drift off to sleep, secure in the Father's embrace.

In the morning prayer blossoms, as gorgeous and unexpected as the flowering of the saguaro. Without bidding, a melody from your youthful days of revelry returns to you. Poetry pours from a source so deep that you have, until now, been unable to tap it. As the hooded lark greets the Lord of the Sunrise, so you sing your praise to the God of Creation and you are sated with gratitude. "The Canticle of Brother Sun" tumbles from your lips:

> Most high, all-powerful, all good, Lord!
>   All praise is yours, all glory, all honor
>   And all blessing.
> To you, alone, Most High, do they belong.
>   No mortal lips are worthy
>   To pronounce your name.
> All praise be yours, my Lord, through all that you have made,
>   And first my lord Brother Sun,
>   Who brings the day; and light you give to us through him.
> How beautiful is he, how radiant in all his splendor!

Your song, Brother Francis, celebrates the God of earth and sky and sea, the God whose only Son called you out of darkness into his glorious light. Your song is sent forth to stir up praise, repentance and thanksgiving in all who hear it. And when at last, Wounded Herald of the Great King, you welcome Sister Death, your song will proclaim your readiness to enter the Kingdom.

Reflection   Although Francis sings of Brother Sun, he is no sunshine saint. His exultant hymn escapes from a body harnessed by blindness and pain. His prayer at a time of constant suffering is pure praise. He evicts self-pity, making room for Christ to sing in him.

At a time of crisis or pain, does my prayer ever turn from petition to praise?

Do I allow illness or frustration to become a deterrent to prayer rather than an impetus to praise?

Praying Like Francis:
San Damiano in My Life

Meditation O my God and my all,
by meditating on the Passion of your Son
I have been fitted for praise. You are Yahweh;
every joy I have ever known has come from you.
Your creation astounds me in its dappled diversity;
I have not yet begun to thank you.

To prepare myself for praise, I will waste time (in my ignorance, I call it that) in looking, just looking at an oak leaf, a robin, a dandelion, a snail, a sleeping cat, a cloud. I will be all eyes, sensing your imprint on every created thing.

How manifold are your works, O LORD!
In wisdom you have wrought them all—
the earth is full of your creatures. (Ps 104:24)

I place myself in a hut at San Damiano, a setting of confinement with a single window on the world. In this school of appreciation, my time is limited. I must learn to overlook the distractions and ignore the frailities that readily consume the hours of light. If I focus myopically on my own troubles, night will cover my head, leaving me in lonely self-contemplation. Teach me, Lord, while there is yet time.

"The light is among you only a little longer.
Walk while you still have it
or darkness will come over you." (Jn 12:35)

Forgetting all but the grandeur of your creation, its awesome complexity and assuring simplicity, its power and order and fearful symmetry, I will become a song of praise. I will sing gratefully from my heart of your goodness to me:

Praise the Lord for all his art and craft and unfathomed
creativity!

For sun-glossed days and distant clouds, cirrus, streamers
and puffs, hailstones, puddles, rainbows and dew.

For winter nights with moon on snow, shadows, wind-
howls and gusts, ice-etch, blizzards, frostwork and
drifts.

For spring planting and garden plot, earthworms,
compost and bees, okra, shallots, cornstalks and sage.

For autumn's harvest and mown hay, barley, buckwheat
and rye, maples, apples, pumpkins and leaves.

For mountain ranges with noble brows, summits, ridges
and bluffs, hummocks, valleys, meadows and leas.

For rolling seas with august surf, salt-spray, whitecaps and
spume, rivers, fountains, runnels and lakes.

For wild creatures of amusing grace: penguins, puffins and
seals, dolphins, pandas, aardvarks and gnus.

For simple beasts that serve us well: Morgans, Guernseys
and shoats, watchdogs, tomcats, oxen and ewes.

For green belts and open spaces, forests, campsites and
parks, sand beaches, playgrounds, islands and zoos.

For diverse nations and many tongues: Russians, Chinese
and Celts, Kenyans, Afghans, Germans and Utes.

For people of faith who worship well: Moslems,
Christians and Sikhs, Buddhists, Confucians, Taoists
and Jews.

Let all who share life praise the Lord for what he has
made. Amen. Alleluia!

Reflection   In harmony with the spirit of Francis, I will extend my
holy leisure by daydreaming about the forms my praise
and gratitude can take:

If I had to name the three persons for whom I am most
grateful, who would they be? How can I praise God for
creating them and leading them into my life?

If I had to name the three possessions for which I am most grateful, what would they be? How can I express my gratitude to the Lord for these things that mean so much to me?

If I had to name the three wounds (setbacks, failures, losses, handicaps) which have been hardest for me to bear, what would they be? Can I now praise God for whatever good may have been accomplished through my suffering?

In what ways am I, like Francis, a wounded herald?

Exploring Further

Response   To internalize the image of the wounded herald, we need
more than the words and attitudes of Francis. Our lives
have to support our prayer as securely as stone buttresses uphold
cathedrals. So how do we begin?

The Peace Prayer of St. Francis provides a blueprint. But
it suffers from over-familiarity. We see it on a greeting card or
sing it at a folk liturgy and file it away with the Pledge of
Allegiance.

Try taking the prayer apart, paraphrasing it, assigning
yourself one line a day to put into practice. Write the line on
your calendar or post it on the refrigerator door. Breathe life into
the beautiful prayer attributed to Francis:

> Lord, make me an instrument of your peace,
> Where there is hatred, let me sow love.
> Where there is injury, pardon.
> Where there is doubt, faith.
> Where there is despair, hope.
> Where there is darkness, light.
> And where there is sadness, joy.
>
> O Divine Master, grant that I may not so much seek
> To be consoled as to console,
> to be understood as to understand,
> to be loved as to love.
> For it is in giving that we receive.
> It is in pardoning that we are pardoned.
> And it is in dying that we are born to eternal life.

Or you might come up with creative forms of praise for
good and bad days. For the former, plan a Franciscan picnic with
simple foods and a Gospel story to "chew on." For the latter,
compose a straight-arrow prayer that doesn't negotiate for instant
relief ("Thanks for the headache, Lord. It has made me sit still
long enough to remember you").

If you're ready for a tougher challenge, try rewarding someone who has wounded your feelings, your reputation, your relationship with another person. The Desert Fathers, hermits of fifth-century Egypt, were masters of this approach:

> There was a certain elder who, if anyone maligned him, would go in person to offer him presents, if he lived nearby. And if he lived at a distance, he would send presents by the hand of another. *(The Wisdom of the Desert,* by Thomas Merton)

To reinforce your relationship with Francis, spend some time with the Gospel passages that shaped his life of prayer:

When you pray...Mt 6:5-6
True riches...Mt 6:19-34
Danger of riches...Mt 19:16-30
Passion and death of Jesus...Mk 15:16-41
The coming of Jesus' hour...Jn 12:23-36

Reading   Deepen your acquaintance with Francis through one of these books:

Francis: The Journey and the Dream, by Murray Bodo (Cincinnati, Ohio: St. Anthony Messenger Press, 1972).
The Perfect Joy of St. Francis, by Felix Timmermans (Garden City: Image Books, 1955).
St. Francis of Assisi, by Morris Bishop (Boston: Little Brown & Co., 1974).
St. Francis of Assisi, edited by Marion A. Habig (Garden City: Image Books, 1955).

CLARE
OF ASSISI
1194-1253

The Anchored Soul

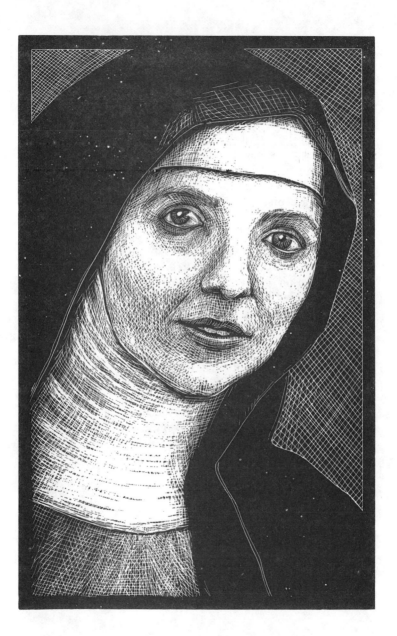

Getting to Know Clare

Life-Sketch   Clare of Assisi is a sign of contradiction. She divests
herself of feminine assets (beauty, wealth, family
connections, eligibility) as eagerly as other women hoard them.
She fights for the "privilege of poverty" as persistently as many
struggle for success in corporate empires. Like her ally, the
charismatic Francis, she upends accepted values, creating
question marks in the minds of complacent Christians.

Her accepted image is the wan and distant Sister Moon
reflecting fiery Francis, Brother Sun. These two medieval saints
of Assisi are as inextricably bound as Mary and Joseph, Benedict
and Scholastica, Francis de Sales and Jane de Chantal. Their
relationship embraces the love of a celibate married couple, of
brother and sister, of friends who complement each other's
spirituality.

Clare is more, however, than a pale reflection of Francis.
She embodies the gospel life he espoused. Hers was the hidden
life of poverty and prayer he would have envied had he not
clearly heard the call to an active ministry. Clare incarnates the
30 years of Jesus' life at Nazareth, a life of daily hardship, simple
joys and restricted horizons.

Her father, Faverone di Offreduccio, was a knight; her
mother, Ortolana, a charitable matron who made pilgrimages to
the Holy Land and to Rome. Their home was a castle where
little Chiara and her sisters learned needlework and music,
reading and writing.

When she was 16, Clare began the secret, chaperoned
meetings with Francis that would sow dissatisfaction with her
comfortable life. He was 28 and had already founded the Friars
Minor and astounded Assisi by his preaching, begging and
inspired foolhardiness. Their ardor for each other was consumed
in their mutual love for Jesus Christ.

In a romantic scene idealized by Franco Zeffirelli in
Brother Sun, Sister Moon, Clare received the rough Franciscan

habit from Francis on the night of Palm Sunday, 1212. That was the beginning of the Second Order, the Poor Ladies, later known as Poor Clares.

After that ecstatic ceremony of self-offering, the young noblewoman apparently never looked back. "I want only Jesus Christ, and to live by the gospel, owning nothing and in chastity," she vowed. For the next 42 years, enclosed in her convent at San Damiano, she lived out that vow in literal poverty and constant prayer.

The Second Order soon attracted many more women who sought to commit themselves to Christ in the contemplative religious life. Clare's compassion and wisdom made her an acclaimed saint in her own time. She and Francis met only rarely; he would not allow himself the pleasure of her company or even of calling her by name. Knight that he was, he felt that the lovely Chiara belonged totally to his Lord.

After Francis' death, Madonna Chiara mothered the friars through the years of transition and did her best to see that the founder's ideals were not compromised. Her reputation as a healer and a spiritual counselor grew.

Among those who confided in her and counted on her prayers were two popes, Gregory IX and Innocent IV. While the former had tried to convince Clare to accept a less rigorous mode of poverty, the latter, at her persistent request, confirmed the "privilege of seraphic poverty" shortly before her death. This pontiff said of her, "She has surpassed all women of her time."

The depth of Clare's union with Christ is evident in a letter she wrote to Agnes of Prague, who founded a monastery of the Second Order in that city:

> His affection holds one fast;
> his contemplation is like a breath of new life.
> His kindness fills one to the brim;
> his sweetness is in overflowing measure.
> The recollection of him shines with a soft light.
> His fragrance revives the dead....
> Now, since he is the splendor of eternal glory

and the brightness of everlasting light
and the mirror without spot (Wis 7:26)...,
look steadfastly into this mirror every day.
See in it every time you look—
and look into it always—
your own face.

(Letter IV, translation by Father David Temple, O.F.M.)

Portrait   Although it is tempting to see Clare as a purely feminine, passive, reflective person, that characterization would be incomplete. Her life at San Damiano was as rigorous as that of any monk or peasant farmer. Raised in a castle, she lived her entire adult life in a small stone convent, slept on a straw mattress, fasted three days a week, never ate meat, often did penance, and got up in the middle of the night to pray the Divine Office. Year around she wore a coarse brown robe with a black veil and went barefoot on stone floors.

Thomas of Celano, her biographer, observed that Clare was of good stature and had an oval face, fine coloring and fair hair. His masculine judgment was that "she inclined to stoutness, but nowise in excess." In early paintings, however, Clare is always tall and slender, perhaps like the candle her name suggested.

Members of her community who testified during the canonization process emphasized the abbess' circumspect leadership: "She often hastened to do herself what she had commanded another to do." They described the humility that led her to wash the extern sisters' feet on their return from a round of begging as well as her love of silence ("Careless speech always weakens our love for God," she insisted). Her devotion to Christ in his Passion was evidenced in all-night vigils and weeping during the hours of the Crucifixion. Chronically ill, she healed others of sickness and depression by signing them with the cross.

Clare called herself the "little plant of the Blessed Francis," and she relied on him as her spiritual director in the early years of her life as a religious. He was wise enough to lead her through a gradual liberation until Christ himself was her only guide. Her devotion toward Francis ripened into a mature love that did not require his physical presence.

In a symbolic vision that underscores the motherly nature of both saints, Clare saw herself climbing a high stairway and carrying a jug of hot water with a towel for Francis. When she reached him, he opened his habit to bare his chest so that she might drink "something sweet and delightful."

While Clare and Francis shared the same gospel insights, she received the gift he desired for himself but which he could enjoy only at intervals: She was the contemplative flowering in a cloister garden, the prayerful person whose daily life was focused on God alone.

Prayer-Life   For the Christian who loves to pray in the direct sense (as opposed to the prayer of pastoral activity, charitable works, evangelization), Clare had an ideal existence. Everything she did was prayer. When she came to San Damiano, says Celano, "There she fixed the anchor of her soul." There she lived in the house of God and God made his dwelling in her. The anchor held fast. She took no vacations, made no pilgrimages, allowed herself no diversions from the single purpose of her life. Like Jesus before his baptism, she lived in obscurity and ordinariness. And she grew in wisdom, age and grace.

The cloister at San Damiano became a source of spiritual energy radiating throughout the Church. Clare and her sisters prayed the Divine Office (Liturgy of the Hours) five times a day, seven days a week, conforming the pattern of their community life to the sequence of the liturgical year. They meditated and kept their silence as habitually as others cling to idle chatter. Washing or scrubbing, weeding or sewing, they were constantly praising God and enjoying his presence.

Speaking of the "liberating gift of enclosure," the Poor Clare *Constitutions* by which Clare's contemporary daughters abide comment, "The enclosed nuns are called to give clear witness that man belongs entirely to God, and so to keep green among the human family the desire for a heavenly home."

31

That evergreen desire is Clare's legacy, not only to contemplatives in cloisters, but to all Christians who recognize in themselves the need to respond regularly to Jesus' invitation: "Whenever you pray, go to your room, close your door, and pray to your Father in private" (Mt 6:6).

Letting Clare Teach Us

Approach We can't all run off to monasteries—although that is a more common temptation than many might guess. Most of us are already anchored in families and jobs or ministries that require us to "go forth" in one way or another. But we do need—and can create—a space for enclosure in our lives. Emulating Clare, we can, according to our circumstances, settle into our personal San Damianos and allow God to monopolize our attention—even if only for a few hours a week.

What characteristics will our contemporary cloisters have? Whether they are indoors or outdoors, behind stone walls or imaginary ones, they will share two essentials: *silence* and a *God-focus*. Everything in them (pine trees and sparrows or candles and a crucifix) should speak to us of God's presence. Anyone or anything else is an intrusion. Let Clare's motto be inscribed over our thresholds: "In God and for God."

While the Abbess of Assisi hasn't left us a journal describing the experience of solitude in her corner cell or her walled garden, a 20th-century contemplative has done so. In *The Sign of Jonas* Thomas Merton writes in terms that Clare, who praised God whenever she saw a tree in leaf or flower in bloom, would welcome:

> My chief joy is to escape to the attic of the garden house and the little broken window that looks out over the valley. There in the silence I love the green grass. The tortured gestures of the apple trees have become part of my prayer....So much do I love this solitude that when I walk out along the road to the old barns that stand alone, far from the new buildings, delight begins to overpower me from head to foot and peace smiles even in the marrow of my bones.

Once anchored in our enclosures, we can pray in whatever manner is most natural to us: vocal prayer, scriptural meditation, the Psalms, the Jesus Prayer, centering—or simple presence, wordless and attentive. Clare would surely advise reflection on the passion and death of Jesus. But for those who feel unable to begin with contemplative prayer, she would point to the Liturgy of the Hours as a fruitful blending of vocal and mental prayer.

Both saints of Assisi had a great love for the Hours as the universal prayer of the Church. The liturgy (Mass and the Divine Office) was the hub of their daily lives; all other work and prayer formed concentric circles around this steady center. Despite her insistence on absolute poverty, Madonna Chiara made certain that each of her daughters had a breviary so that she might be intimately familiar with the annual cycle of Psalms, readings and prayers.

The Hours, as they were offered by Clare's Poor Ladies and other monastic orders, followed a centuries-old pattern:

Matins and Lauds (middle of the night),
Prime and Terce (early morning),
Sext and None (noon, early afternoon),
Vespers (late afternoon),
Compline (early evening).

In *The Constitution on the Sacred Liturgy,* Vatican Council II called for revising and modernizing the Hours, emphasizing that the new breviaries should be available to *all* the people of God. Lay men and women were encouraged to adapt the ancient liturgical prayer to their varied life-styles. The new rite provides morning, midday and evening Hours harmonized with the liturgical year. It is a readily accessible and desirable resource for anyone who seeks structure and communal significance for daily prayer.

Consideration Can Clare's willingness to accept permanent enclosure out of love for Christ prompt us to welcome temporary enclosure for the same reason?

Are we serious enough about improving our prayer life to create and be faithful to a cloister of our own choosing?

Might we follow Clare's lead and explore the Liturgy of
the Hours as a possible form of everyday prayer?

Invocation   Madonna Chiara,
Pope Alexander IV called you
a "lofty candlestick of holiness
that burned brightly in the tabernacle of the Lord."
Burn brightly before me now,
that I may see you at San Damiano
and learn the value of enclosure.
Intercede for me
that my restive spirit may gladly settle in one sacred place
where God can be "the meaning of my hours."
Let the light of Christ,
shining through you,
illumine my way.
Clare-candle, burn brightly. Amen.

Praying With Clare:
San Damiano in Early Morning

Meditation   As the sun slowly rises to run its course, the Valley of
Spoleto shakes off the darkness that has held it in thrall.
The swallows find their voices and remember their songs. Mount
Subasio emerges in the distance, a slumberous giant comforted by
clouds. Light wakens the olive trees and bathes the cypresses.

The stones of San Damiano, set in place by Francis in his
zeal to repair his Lord's church, announce the stability of the
lives they now shelter. This is a sacred place, a place where the
Lord need never ask, "But when the Son of Man comes, will he
find any faith on the earth?" (Lk 18:8).

In a narrow corner cell, the Abbess of San Damiano is
absorbing the sunrise. Seated by the window, she feels her unity
with the swallows, the olive trees, the mountain. They are of one

purpose: "in God and for God." They are entirely occupied with him.

Clare's face portrays serenity. The intensity of her years of prayer and penance has raised her to a plateau beyond anxiety and disturbance. Even the invading Saracens, having scaled the convent walls, were turned back by her confident prayer for protection. She knew that Christ would never allow his Poor Ladies to fall prey to the marauders. Nor would he allow San Damiano to be violated.

This chapel-convent had been Francis' gift to Jesus and Jesus' gift to Clare. Hadn't the Poverello predicted, as he lugged and lifted the stones, that "there will dwell therein Ladies by whose marvelous and holy living the Lord will be glorified throughout his Church"?

She remembers coming to San Damiano, her joy in the anticipation of a centered life. "And there she fixed the anchor of her soul." The anchor is always there to tug her back if she daydreams of going off to St. Mary of the Angels to see Francis, or to her childhood home to visit her relatives. If she is tempted to travel to other monasteries to help her beloved Agnes or Ermentrude, the anchor will hold her fast. The hidden life of Nazareth, once entered, cannot be set aside.

Reflecting on the meaning of enclosure, she turns the familiar symbols over in her mind, letting the light penetrate them. Before all else, enclosure is like Mary's womb where the Word was confined by the immensity of his love. "She carried him in the little cloister of her womb," Clare thinks, identifying with the pregnant Mary carrying God-With-Us. Woman and Word were woven and welded together, held captive by their absolute need to fulfill the Father's longing.

Enclosure is like the narrow manger that cradled Emmanuel, the rough wood that enthroned the newborn Prince of Peace. That straw-filled manger welcomed the Mighty One, who willingly consented to such boundaries for his limitlessness. He who might have moved wherever he would among the planets or over the waters or beyond the mountains imprisoned himself in flesh and manger. He took upon himself the confines of our humanness.

Again, enclosure is like the home of Joseph the carpenter in Nazareth, a humble place without social distinction or spaciousness. In that home the Son of God made himself subject to parental guidance and correction, living what must have seemed to others a poor existence in an insignificant town. There he lived even into his manhood, without wife or respectable profession, accomplishing nothing of worldly import. Jesus remained hidden, content to be his mother's companion and his Father's devoted Son. His hour had not yet come.

And when his hour did come, Clare reflects, enclosure became that cramped circle at the foot of the cross, bounded by armed guards and jeering bystanders. Enclosure was the place where the Marys and John stood, trying to shield Jesus with the cloak of their compassion, ready to receive his stiffening body into their pliant arms. Clare too has stood there, time after time, washing the ignominy from the place with her tears.

"Keep your eyes fast on him who for you was reckoned of no account and let your part be to be willing to be held of no account for him," she advised her daughters. In this enclosure the flame of her devotion has often burned throughout the night as she spends herself in adoration.

Clare surveys her cell: the straw mattress, the washbasin, the crucifix. At times this cell, like the cloister itself, becomes a tabernacle in which Jesus makes himself at home. Then this slender space encompasses the universe and holds all that she could ever desire. Anchored in the sea of his tenderness, she can only "behold him, consider him, contemplate him and desire to imitate him."

Reflection   When a place has been set aside for the solitary purpose of prayer and when it has been resorted to with fidelity over a period of time, even the walls themselves begin to speak of God. He takes possession of the place and the one who occupies it.

Have I ever experienced such a place?

How do I feel about the words *cloister* and *enclosure*?

What is my attitude toward religious recluses and hermits? Are they contributing anything to society?

Praying Like Clare: A Place to Drop Anchor

Meditation   Brother Jesus,
             through your radiant Chiara
             you have reminded me of my need
             to anchor my soul in a place of prayer,
             a place where we can come together
             to worship the Father.
             Free me from my restless activity,
             my slavery to the clock,
             my habit of bobbing along on the open sea
             when you have called me to be still.
             When I consider how you consented to enclosure
             in Mary's womb,
             in a narrow manger,
             in a carpenter's home,
             on the wooden cross,
             in the bread of Eucharist,
             my heart is moved to seek enclosure with you. Amen.

I picture myself in a cloister of my own making or choosing. Whether it is indoors or outdoors, I can feel at home there with you. It is a place that is accessible to me every day or a few times a week. In selecting my sacred space, I fully intend to be faithful to it. It is not simply a pleasant retreat into which I will withdraw when the mood strikes me.

Jesus, I see you cradled in a manger, swaddled against the cold, confined by the poverty you have chosen. By being born among the *anawim*, you have accepted the limitations of those who have neither wealth nor power, respect nor authority. Have you begun to feel the frustrations of all people whom society judges to be of no account? Do you cry "Abba!" for the poor, the refugee, the outcast, the hungry? Do you dream yet of the day when you can heal and feed and console and free the forgotten ones? Do you intercede with the Father for those who are confined by their lowliness?

> He raises up the lowly from the dust;
>> from the dunghill he lifts up the poor
> To seat them with princes,
>> with the princes of his own people. (Ps 113:7-8)

I sit or kneel in silence, breathing expansively and relaxing any tensions in my body. A scented candle or incense can awaken my senses to your presence, Jesus. (I remember Clare's perception: "His fragrance revives the dead.") Outside, I can find your fragrance in apple trees or balsam branches, clover or sea breezes.

When I close my eyes, I shut the door to my inner room and am ready to pray to my Father in private.

Jesus, I see you afloat in Mary's womb, subjecting yourself to nature's nine-month confinement. Do you long to break out, to kick free, to relieve your mother of the burden? Do you feel the frustration of the imprisoned and the invalid? Do you cry "Abba!" for those enclosed against their will? Do you dream of the Spirit who moves abroad, quickening all creatures with the divine breath? Do you contemplate the Father? I hear Clare's words:

> Behold him,
> consider him,
> contemplate him
> and desire to imitate him.

Jesus, I see you at home in Nazareth, your greatness hidden in the ordinariness of daily routines. You are enclosed in your identity as the son of Mary and Joseph the carpenter, confined by the leisurely pace of maturation and by parental expectations for an only child. Do you feel the frustration of all children who, longing to please, often irritate or offend without knowing? Do you cry "Abba!" for teenagers trapped between dependence and self-determination? Do you dream of opening our eyes to the reality of liberation in spiritual childhood?

> I offer you praise, O Father,
> Lord of heaven and earth,
> because what you have hidden
> from the learned and the clever
> you have revealed to the merest children. (Lk 10:21)

Jesus, I see you suspended from the cross, held implacably by heavy-hammered nails, confined by blind hatred and perverse injustice. Can anyone be more cloistered than you, isolated between heaven and earth, separated from angels and men? Enclosed in agony, you do not cry "Abba!" Alone and shaken by that unexpected solitude, you cry, "My God, my God, why have you forsaken me?" (Mk 15:34), as though you are no longer sure that *Abba* and *Eloi,* Father and God, are one.

Do you grieve for those who are confined by the threatening approach of a painful death? For those bound by brutal torturers? Do you dream of sunrise-resurrection and shared homecoming?

> "I am indeed going to prepare a place for you,
> and then I shall come back to take you with me,
> that where I am you also may be." (Jn 14:3)

Jesus, I see you cloistered in the Eucharist, circumscribed by the humbleness of bread. What greater love has any person than that which is eager to be ground, pressed down and broken for one's friends?

When you enter my tabernacle, do you find space and peace, love and awareness? Do you find one willing to be held fast by your affection and filled to the brim by your kindness? Sweet, splendid Jesus, let it be.

Reflection Enclosure can mean fulfillment or frustration, tranquility or restiveness. Our experience of a temporary cloister will be determined by our perception of its purpose. Is it a place where we go to shut out the world and seek satisfaction in prayer? A cozy retreat where Jesus dispenses peace of mind and consoling thoughts? If charity and penance do not accompany us into the cell, we will simply imprison ourselves in self-will.

As Clare of Assisi taught, enclosure must enlarge the heart with caring for those who do not pray, who do no penance, who fail to recognize their need for God. It must foster compassion for those who are crucified by wickedness.

Intercessory prayer is as much a priority for the lay contemplative as it is for the Poor Clare or Trappist monk. Otherwise, we ignore the example of our Teacher, "Christ Jesus…who is at the right hand of God and who intercedes for us" (Rom 8:34).

Penance can be prayer's companion when we anchor our souls despite fatigue, depression, ill-temper, a hectic schedule, faltering faith. When we come into our sacred place to do the will of the One who sent us rather than to please ourselves, we can expect meaningful prayer.

What are my motives in considering enclosure?

Is my prayer sagging for lack of penance?

Praying With Clare:
Morning Prayer in the Chapel

Meditation   Clare and her sisters have gathered in the chapel for
                morning prayer. They stand in two rows facing each other
across the aisle, brown-robed and black-veiled, their faces framed
in white. They are about to pray the Office of the Passion
composed by St. Francis and favored by Madonna Chiara. In it
praises culled from the Scriptures and from Francis' fertile prayer
life precede a mosaic of phrases from the Psalms. The Office
concludes with the Doxology and a blessing.

        The nuns recite rather than sing the Office. * You may
decide to join them—or just listen. They begin with an Our
Father, slowly paced, and then commence the dialogue:

> THE PRAISES
>
> "Holy, holy, holy, is the Lord God Almighty,
>   He who was, and who is, and who is to come!" (Rev 4:8)
>
> *Let us praise and glorify him forever!*
>
> "O Lord our God, you are worthy
>   to receive glory and honor and power!" (Rev 4:11)
>
> *Let us praise and glorify him forever!*
>
> "Worthy is the Lamb that was slain
>   to receive power and riches, wisdom and strength,
>   honor and glory and praise!" (Rev 5:12)
>
> *Let us praise and glorify him forever!*
>
> Let us bless the Father and the Son and the Holy Spirit.
>
> *Let us praise and glorify him forever!*
>
> "Bless the Lord, all you works of the Lord,
>   praise and exalt him above all forever." (Dan 3:57)

---

* Adapted from "Writings of St. Francis," *St. Francis of Assisi:*
Omnibus of Sources, edited by Marion A. Habig (Chicago:
Franciscan Herald Press, 1972).

Let us praise and glorify him forever!

"Praise our God, all you his servants,
  the small and the great, who revere him!" (Rev 19:5)

Let us praise and glorify him forever!

Praise him in his glory, heaven and earth,
and "every creature in heaven
and on earth and under the earth
and in the sea;
everything in the universe...." (Rev 5:13)

Let us praise and glorify him forever!

Glory be to the Father,
and to the Son,
and to the Holy Spirit.

Let us praise and glorify him forever!

As it was in the beginning,
is now.
and ever shall be,
world without end. Amen.

Let us praise and glorify him forever!

Let us pray: Almighty, most holy, most high and supreme God, highest good, all good, wholly good, who alone are good: To thee we render all praise, all glory, all thanks, all honor, all blessing, and we shall always refer all good to thee. Amen.

THE PSALMS

Antiphon:
Holy Virgin Mary, there is none like you born in the world among women, daughter and handmaid of the most high King, the heavenly Father.

Have pity on me, O God; for men trample upon me;
  all the day they press their attack against me.
My adversaries trample upon me all the day;
  yes, many fight against me. (Ps 56:2-3)

All my foes whisper against me;
  against me they imagine the worst.... (Ps 41:8)

> ...They who keep watch against my life keep
> counsel together. (Ps 71:10b)

> When one comes to see me, he speaks without sincerity;
> his heart stores up malice;
> when he leaves he gives voice to it outside. (Ps 41:7)

> But I am a worm, not a man;
> the scorn of men, despised by the people. (Ps 22:7)

> For all my foes I am an object of reproach,
> a laughingstock to my neighbors,
> and a dread to my friends.... (Ps 31:12)

> But you, O LORD, be not far from me;
> O my help, hasten to aid me. (Ps 22:20)

> Make haste to help me,
> O Lord my salvation! (Ps 38:23)

> Glory be to the Father, and to the Son, and to the Holy Spirit:
> As it was in the beginning, is now, and ever shall be, world
> without end. Amen.

> Let us pray: Let us bless the Lord God, living and true; let us
> refer praise, glory, honor, blessing and all praise to him always.
> Amen. Amen. So be it!

Clare and her sisters now kneel facing the altar above which hangs the crucifix from which Jesus spoke to Francis. The face of Christ, with its beautiful dark eyes, is calm as he sees beyond present suffering to eternal beatitude. This face holds promises too wonderful to grasp, joys too transcendant to be held in the mind. The sisters remain in silence, caught up in their contemplative gaze at their beloved.

After a while the abbess rouses herself and leads the community in the prayer Francis always offered before this crucifix:

> Great God of all glory and you my Lord Jesus Christ,
> I beseech you to illuminate me
> and to dissipate the darkness of my spirit,
> to give me a pure faith, firm hope and perfect charity.

44

O my God, grant me to know you well
and to do all things according to your light
and in conformity with your most holy will. Amen.

Reflection   In liturgical prayer, we make the words of Scripture and
the petitions of the Church our own. Like any other
vocal prayer, the Hours are empty repetition if they are not
offered with what Francis termed "a harmony of words and
hearts."

Do the Psalms appeal to me as a source of prayer?

Which Psalms in particular speak in a voice that I can
recognize as my own?

What difficulties, if any, do I have with formal, liturgical
prayer?

How might these difficulties be solved?

Praying Like Clare: Liturgy of the Hours

Meditation   In a lyric scene in which the young Clare anticipates her
life at San Damiano, Mother Mary Francis, P.C.C., gives
her the following lines:

Agnes, for this pray God: that Messer Francis
Find me a little plot in God's broad acres
And plant me there where God alone shall see
My face. And God alone shall be the meaning
Of all my hours. (*Candle in Umbria*, I, 1)

How can I—a homemaker, professional, artist or
craftsman, factory worker, retired person, grocery clerk—have
any relationship with a cloistered religious woman of the 13th

century? How can God be the meaning of all my hours?

Clare had the advantage and the adversity of total enclosure. In a clear and direct sense her life could be God-centered. I cannot imitate her. Just as I *interpret* the message of Jesus' life (rather than *copy* its physical essentials), I look to you, Holy Spirit, for guidance in discerning what the witness of Clare should mean to me. I consider whether her devotion to the Hours has relevance in my life.

As Clare prayed the Franciscan Office of the Passion, I turn to the contemporary liturgy of the Triumph of the Cross (September 14) for excerpts from Evening Prayer. I enter my enclosure and prepare, mentally and physically, for adoration.

> *Opening Prayer:*
> God come to my assistance.
>   Lord, make haste to help me.
> Glory to the Father, and to the Son, and to the Holy Spirit:
> as it was in the beginning, is now, and will be for ever.
>   Amen. Alleluia.

> HYMN

> *(Sing or listen to any appropriate song, such as "If I Be Lifted Up," "Song of Jesus Christ" or "Were You There?")*

> PSALMODY

> *Antiphon:*
> Our crucified and risen Lord has redeemed us, alleluia.

> Praise the LORD, for he is good;
>   sing praise to our God, for he is gracious;
>   it is fitting to praise him.

> The LORD rebuilds Jerusalem;
>   the dispersed of Israel he gathers.
> He heals the brokenhearted
>   and binds up their wounds.
> He tells the number of the stars;
>   he calls each by name.

> Great is our Lord and mighty in power:

to his wisdom there is no limit.
The LORD sustains the lowly;
    the wicked he casts to the ground.

Sing to the LORD with thanksgiving;
    sing praise with the harp to our God,
Who covers the heavens with clouds,
    who provides rain for the earth;
Who makes grass sprout on the mountains
    and herbs for the service of men;
Who gives food to the cattle,
    and to the young ravens when they cry to him.

In the strength of the steed he delights not,
    nor is he pleased with the fleetness of men.
The LORD is pleased with those who fear him,
    with those who hope for his kindness. (Ps 147:1-11)

CANTICLE

Antiphon:
We must glory in the cross of our Lord Jesus Christ.

Though he was in the form of God,
    he did not deem equality with God
    something to be grasped at.

Rather, he emptied himself
    and took the form of a slave,
    being born in the likeness of men.

He was known to be of human estate,
    and it was thus that he humbled himself,
    obediently accepting even death,
    death on a cross!

Because of this,
    God highly exalted him
    and bestowed on him the name
    above every other name,

So that at Jesus' name
    every knee must bend
    in the heavens, on the earth,
    and under the earth,
    and every tongue proclaim

to the glory of God the Father:
JESUS CHRIST IS LORD! (Phil 2:6-11)

READING

…We preach Christ crucified—a stumbling block to Jews, and an absurdity to Gentiles; but to those who are called, Jews and Greeks alike, Christ the power of God and the wisdom of God.
(1 Cor 1:23-24)

Responsory:
This sign will appear in the heavens when the Lord comes.
Lift up your heads, your salvation is at hand.
    When the Lord comes.
Glory to the Father….
    This sign will appear in the heavens when the Lord comes.

CANTICLE OF MARY

Antiphon:
It was ordained that Christ should suffer, and on the third day rise from the dead.

"My being proclaims the greatness of the Lord,
    my spirit finds joy in God my savior,

For he has looked upon his servant in her lowliness;
    all ages to come shall call me blessed.

God who is mighty has done great things for me,
    holy is his name;

His mercy is from age to age
    on those who fear him.

He has shown might with his arm;
    he has confused the proud in their inmost thoughts.

He has deposed the mighty from their thrones
    and raised the lowly to high places.

The hungry he has given every good thing,
    while the rich he has sent empty away.

He has upheld Israel his servant,
    ever mindful of his mercy;

Even as he promised our fathers,

promised Abraham and his descendants forever."

(Lk 1:47-55)

INTERCESSIONS

Let us pray with confidence to Christ who endured the cross to
save us.
Lord, through your cross bring us to the glory of your
Kingdom.

O Christ, you emptied yourself, taking the form of a servant and
being made like us,
grant that your people may follow the example of your
humility.

O Christ, you humbled yourself and became obedient unto
death, even death on a cross,
grant that your servants may imitate your obedience and
willing acceptance of trials.

O Christ, you were raised up by the Father and given the name
that is above all other names,
may your people, strengthened in the hope of a heavenly
resurrection, persevere to the end.

O Christ, at your name every knee in heaven, on earth and
under the earth will bend in adoration,
pour out your love upon all men that they may join together
in proclaiming your glory.

O Christ, every tongue shall confess that you are Lord to the
glory of God the Father,
welcome our brothers and sisters who have died into the
unfailing joy of your Kingdom.

(*Add your own petitions.*)

Our Father...

May the Lord bless us,
protect us from all evil
and bring us to everlasting life.
Amen.

Reflection   According to the *Constitution on the Sacred Liturgy*, the
Hours are "a source of devotion and nourishment for

personal prayer" (#90). They provide us with a self-imposed
discipline against the aimlessness of "I never have time to pray"
or "I don't really feel that I know how to pray." They prompt
growth in prayer by enriching us with daily Psalms and readings
from the Bible, the saints and modern spiritual writers.

Am I willing to experiment with the Liturgy of the Hours
as a cure for the scattershot-spirituality of praying now
and then or occasionally reading a Scripture passage?

As I honestly assess my prayer life, do I find any good
reasons for not exploring the possibilities of enclosure and
the Hours?

Exploring Further

Response　In responding to the prayerful life of Clare of Assisi, we
will have to work out whatever patterns our own lives can
accommodate. We may find enclosure in a loft, a spare room, a
garden, a rooftop, a tree house, an attic—wherever we can
anchor ourselves out of distraction's way.

If we are lucky enough to find a place that is simple and
silent, a place where "peace smiles even in the marrow of our
bones," we will have little trouble in remaining faithful to it.
Jesus soon shares his appetite for solitude with us.

The Liturgy of the Hours is available in numerous
editions that range from seasonal booklets to four leatherbound
volumes encompassing the entire three-year liturgical cycle.
Here is a sampling of the possibilities:

> *Daytime Prayer* (United States Catholic Conference,
> Washington, D.C.). Morning prayer with condensed
> readings to be used at midmorning, midday and
> midafternoon. Modest price.
>
> *Christian Prayer: The Liturgy of the Hours* (Liturgical
> Press, Collegeville, Minn.). Morning and evening
> prayer with Office of Readings for liturgical year.
> Available in basic edition as well as a slightly more
> expensive version with musical settings. Moderate
> price.
>
> *Liturgy of the Hours* (Catholic Book Publishing Co., New
> York). The official edition selected by the U.S.
> Bishops' Committee on the Liturgy. Complete office in
> four volumes. Expensive.
>
> *Christian Prayer* (Catholic Book Publishing Co., New
> York). Official one-volume edition with morning and
> evening prayer. Moderate price.
>
> *Morning Praise and Evensong* (Fides Publishers, Notre
> Dame, Ind.). For parishes and emerging Christian

communities—which might describe you and a few
friends—this version of morning and evening prayer
adapts the Hours to musical settings. Helpful
suggestions on liturgical aids to enhance the Hours as
a prayerful experience. Modest price.

Advent Evening Prayer (Federation of Diocesan Liturgical
Commissions, Chicago, Ill.). Excellent resource for
those who want to experiment with a seasonal, partial
liturgy. Inexpensive.

Finally, to strengthen your relationship with Clare of
Assisi, spend some time in your enclosure reflecting on the
following Scripture passages:

On prayer...Mt 6:5-8, 19
On poverty...Mt 19:16-24
The Passion...Mt 27
Martha and Mary...Lk 11:38-42
On spiritual maturity...Phil 3:7-16
Christ lives in me...Gal 2:19-21
A prayerful person...Ps 119:145-149

Reading Enter more deeply into Clare's enclosure with one of
these books:

Candle in Umbria: The Story of St. Clare of Assisi, by Sr. Mary
Francis (Roswell, New Mexico: Poor Clare Monastery of Our
Lady of Guadalupe, 1953).

Clare: A Light in the Garden, by Murray Bodo (Cincinnati: St.
Anthony Messenger Press, 1979).

The Legend and Writings of St. Clare of Assisi, edited by Ignatius
Brady (St. Bonaventure, New York: The Franciscan Institute,
1953).

St. Clare of Assisi, by Nesta DeRobeck (Chicago: Franciscan
Herald Press, 1980).

St. Francis of Assisi: Omnibus of Sources, edited by Marion A.
Habig (Chicago: Franciscan Herald Press, 1973).

IGNATIUS OF LOYOLA
1491-1556

The Sensual Christian

Getting to Know Ignatius

Life-Sketch   If Ignatius of Loyola is judged by the stereotypes that cling
like barnacles to the order he founded, he emerges
looking like a combination of General George Patton and
theologian Hans Kung. Mention the Jesuits and minds
automatically register *militancy, intellectualism, education of the
elite.*

How could the sire of the Society of Jesus be anything but
an unbending scourge of heretics, a mastermind of muscular
spirituality, a mystic whose brilliance was beyond the ken of
ordinary Christians? Like John of the Cross, Ignatius seems to
occupy a realm of upper-class sanctity with as much popular
appeal as astrophysics.

In fact, the author of the famed *Spiritual Exercises* has less
in common with his fellow Spaniard John than he has with
Francis of Assisi. Son of a well-to-do family, Iñigo spent his
youth in pursuit of pleasure, dueling and living up to the image of
a dashing *caballero.* He described himself as a man who "took a
special delight in the exercise of arms, with a great and vain
desire of winning glory." He shared Francis' affection for fine
apparel, admiring himself in feathered caps, luxurious capes and
fitted leggings.

While fighting in the service of the Duke of Najera in
1521, Ignatius was wounded at Pamplona. Although his leg was
shattered, his vanity was unharmed. He insisted on a second
excruciating operation to reset the leg to avoid an unsightly
protruberance. He decided to undergo this martyrdom to gratify
his own inclinations, he later told his biographer Luis Gonzalez
de Camara.

During his long recuperation, Iñigo had to bide his time
with reading—an occupation he rarely indulged in when well.
The library in the family castle provided a life of Christ and some
romanticized biographies of the saints. The young soldier, whose
allegiance to the Church was innocent of spiritual depth, began

to see that there was more to life than *amor y victoria.*
In time, his military heroes were toppled by Francis and
Dominic, whose spiritual prowess challenged his imagination.
For perhaps the first time in his life, he began to pray with
regularity. He had a vision of Mary holding her holy child and,
after that, he was overtaken by disgust at the exploits of his past.

When his leg had healed, Ignatius made a pilgrimage to
Montserrat where he kept a night-long vigil before Our Lady's
statue. In the morning, he abandoned his sword at her altar and
exchanged his finery for a pilgrim's tunic. Like Francis before
him, he saw himself as a knight of Christ. His conversion bore a
remarkable harvest within a year when, out of a retreat at
Manresa, came the first draft of the *Spiritual Exercises,* a manual
of prayer and interior renewal.

Ignatius' fierce desire for penance, solitude and service
soon led him into the realm of contemplative prayer. He
experienced a mystical illumination of God's pervading presence
in creation, seeing the world from above as though he shared the
Creator's vision. This powerful insight into our total dependence
on God and our need for Christ as the mediator between heaven
and earth characterized his teaching throughout his religious life.

After making a pilgrimage to Jerusalem, Ignatius returned
to school so that he might become a more profitable servant. At
the age of 33, he attended classes with 10-year-old boys, a
humiliation his once-proud spirit took in stride. When he wasn't
studying, he was begging and preaching in one town or another.
He went on to the universities of Alcala, Salamanca and Paris,
gathering confreres along the way.

His preaching on the *Exercises* was judged heretical by
certain Church authorities who accused him of misleading people
on the matter of mortal and venial sin. They were, in truth,
more concerned about rumors that he had sent two women (one
the beautiful and charming daughter of the other) off on foot
alone as pilgrims to the shrine at Jaen. Ignatius was imprisoned
until the women returned, months later, to verify his story that
he had advised them to stay home in Alcala and serve the poor

instead of wandering through the countryside where they might be robbed or abducted.

Although he was exonerated, Ignatius was ordered not to preach on the distinction between mortal and venial sin until he was academically qualified to do so. The restriction was imposed even though the author of the *Exercises* had satisfactorily answered all his accusers' questions. Incidents like this one contributed to his progress in throttling egoism and shedding the burden of self-importance.

Ignatius worked and begged his way through the universities until, at age 43, he received his master's degree. By then he had a nucleus of followers who wanted to form a religious community dedicated to reform of the Church through preaching, teaching and missionary activity. Three years later, when Ignatius was ordained in Venice in 1537, the community took the formal name of the Society of Jesus. While they were on their way to Rome to offer their services to the pope, the founder had an affirming vision of Christ, who promised that the new order would be approved.

In record time the remarkable Jesuits made a name for themselves throughout Europe as brilliant opponents of heresy, proponents of the sacramental life and preeminent teachers. Their lives reflected the watchwords of Ignatian spirituality: *freedom* and *service*. The founder was adamant in his belief that there is "no greater mistake in spiritual matters than to force others to follow one's own pattern." Both the *Exercises* and the Jesuit *Constitutions* foster freedom from self-serving attachments, as well as a desire to do Christ's work in the world.

We can hear this theme echoing in a familiar Ignatian prayer:

> Accept, O Lord, all my freedom.
> Accept my memory, my mind, and all my will.
> Whatever I am or possess,
> you have graciously given me;
> I give it all back to you,
> to be completely governed by your will.

> Give me only your love and your grace
> and I am rich enough,
> and I ask nothing more.

Portrait　Ignatius succeeded at the balancing act that his
commitment to freedom and service, contemplation and
action required of him. At times, the price he paid was high.
Bouts of scrupulosity and depression drained him of the
conviction that he was fulfilling Christ's call. Illness and
persecution of his sons also took their toll. But charity and
humor rescued him from difficulties that might otherwise have
appeared too much to bear.

When a rival religious threatened to burn every Jesuit he
found between Perpignan and Seville, Ignatius wrote him a letter
recommending that not only should the Jesuits between
Perpignan and Seville be burned, but Ignatius and all his friends
and acquaintances "throughout the whole world should be
enkindled and inflamed by the Holy Spirit."

The saint's portrait reveals the firm features and
expressive eyes of one who has seen through the facade of worldly
concerns to the reality of Christ's Kingdom on earth. His
contemporaries knew him as a man of strong will, empathy and
spiritual insight. He was remembered for his habit of praising
someone whom others had insulted, for his composure under fire,
for his witness to the necessity of taming the tongue. He asked of
no one what he himself was unwilling to do.

The expansion of the Jesuits during Ignatius' lifetime
proved him an able administrator who understood how to draw
the best out of his followers—many of whom became heroes of
the Church in their own right (Francis Xavier, Francis Borgia,
Peter Faber). His every decision was guided by a single final
question: Will God be glorified? His directives to his sons were
given "in our Lord"—a phrase they sometimes tired of hearing
with such regularity—and in conformity with the motto: *Ad
Majoram Dei Gloriam* ("To the Greater Glory of God").

To a greater degree than many mystics, Ignatius insisted

on the necessity of apostolic action as a direct consequence of contemplation. Authentic meditation, he felt, would be impossible for the person who was not fully prepared to apply the fruits of prayer to service: "I understand in order that I may act."

The knight of Christ could not retreat to an ivory tower, leaving others to wage the Divine Majesty's campaigns. He must enlist mind and heart in the active work of redemption—a responsibility not only of Jesuits but of all Christians.

Prayer-Life   Ignatius shared with Francis of Assisi a deeply contemplative view of creation. He saw God's works as though they were illuminated from within, showing forth their true nature and value. He experienced (not just knew about or believed in) the divine presence with an immediacy granted to few saints. His senses drank fully of this presence which intoxicated him with intensified awareness.

"At the sight of a little plant, a leaf, a flower or a fruit, an insignificant worm or a tiny animal, Ignatius could soar free above the heavens and reach through into things which lie beyond the senses," wrote his biographer Pedro de Ribadeneira. What is so often opaque to us was transparent to him. He saw the world as it really is: full of Christ and fully reliant on Christ.

In the person of Jesus he recognized the focal point of creation, the convergence of divinity and humanity, the vibrant link between God and us. Ignatius, like St. Paul, saw Christ coming down from the Father to lift us up through his death on the cross: "You are well acquainted with the favor shown you by our Lord Jesus Christ: how for your sake he made himself poor though he was rich, so that you might become rich by his poverty" (2 Cor 8:9).

The spirituality of Ignatius, as codified in his *Exercises,* reflects his belief that our senses can provide us with passage into the mysteries of Christ's life. They can enable us to experience the history of salvation in the present tense.

An Ignatian retreatant isn't satisfied with *thinking about* the Passion; he or she must be *present* at the Crucifixion, alive to the sights, sounds, smells and feelings of the event. Merely to read the *Exercises* is to miss the boat. Ignatius demands involvement of the whole person.

In contrast to Therese of Lisieux's no-method approach to prayer, the *Exercises* are a carefully-organized regimen. They require a commitment to follow Ignatius' training program and to allow him, through a spiritual director or retreat master, to do the coaching.

The ideal setting is a month-long retreat away from familiar surroundings—a luxury few of us can afford. Within recent years, however, the *Exercises* have been adapted to various circumstances (at-home retreats, weekends at Christian Life Centers, evenings of reflection) and made more accessible to people seeking renewal, guidance in prayer, or enlightenment in decision-making.

The *Exercises* are designed to lead the retreatant toward freedom and service through meditative prayer and some form of fasting. Gradually, he or she reaches the point where decisions can be based on love of God rather than personal attachments. Decisions about marriage partners, business opportunities, career changes, possible ministries, family problems can then be swayed by the spirit of the gospel rather than impelled by the spirit of ambition, possessiveness or pride.

Based on a four-week succession of meditations, the *Exercises* open with a consideration of God's love and our own sinfulness, our refusal to respond to that love. They then move on to reflection on the life of Christ, his suffering and death, his resurrection and his presence in our renewed world. Each day's pattern includes *preparation for prayer* (developing reverence and daily integration); *grace* (seeking a spiritual gift); *directed meditation* enlisting the senses; a closing *Our Father.*

As a supplement to the daily exercise, Ignatius recommended self-squelching penances. Here he was in harmony with Therese, who recognized the cumulative power derived from denial of small pleasures.

Contemporary Ignatian directors advise us to fast by

eating less, sleeping less and willingly taking on discomfort as a means of toning up our spirituality. Again, Ignatius takes his cue from Paul in reminding us, "…whether you eat or drink— whatever you do—you should do all for the glory of God" (1 Cor 10:31).

Despite his preference for an orderly progression in the *Exercises,* the author was flexible in his advice about the forms prayer might take for the individual. He counseled Jesuit scholastics to avoid long and tiring meditation, urging them instead to seek God in the enjoyment of landscapes, good conversation, pleasant walks and other pursuits that exercise the senses. "Everything that one turns in the direction of God," he said, "is prayer."

Letting Ignatius Teach Us

Approach   Ignatius challenges us to be sensual Christians. He wants
us to enflesh prayer by bringing our bodily senses to bear
on the Scriptures. His approach reminds us that Jesus was a
distinctively sensual person who never missed a chance to appeal
to the sight and hearing, touch and taste of his listeners in order
to awaken them to the significance of the ordinary and forge
links between the human and the divine:

> You are the salt of the earth. (Mt 5:13)
>
> Look at the birds in the sky....(Mt 6:26)
>
> The reign of God is like yeast....(Mt 13:33)
>
> Blest are your ears because they hear. (Mt 13:16)
>
> How often I have yearned to gather your children, as a mother
> bird gathers her young under her wings....(Mt 24:37)
>
> Do you remember the five loaves among five thousand and how
> many baskets-full you picked up?" (Mt 16:9)
>
> Take this and eat....(Mt 26:26)

The Gospels are abloom with evidence that Jesus touched
people—not just with his words, but with his hands, his physical
presence. He was angry with his disciples when they tried to
prevent the children from crowding around him. "Then he
embraced them and blessed them, placing his hands on them"
(Mk 10:16).

He healed the deaf-mute by dramatically sharing his own
acute senses with the handicapped one. "...He put his fingers
into the man's ears and, spitting, touched his tongue; then he
looked up to heaven and emitted a groan. He said to him,
'*Ephphatha!*' (that is, 'Be opened!')" (Mk 7:33-34).

After driving the evil spirit from the possessed boy, Jesus
"took him by the hand and helped him to his feet" (Mk 9:27).

And when the penitent woman washed his feet with her

tears, perfumed them with expensive oil and dried them with her hair, Jesus was consoled by such extravagant attention. "You gave me no kiss," he reprimanded his host, Simon the Pharisee, "but she has not ceased kissing my feet since I entered" (Lk 7:45).

Like Jesus, the sensual Christian enjoys being embraced, touched, healed, helped, held, kissed. Too often we lock these appeals to our senses out of our prayer, as though prayer were a purely mental process or an activity of the disembodied soul. If we remember Jesus in Gethsemani, the most detailed description we have of him at prayer, we can not doubt that he prayed with his whole person.

Ignatius, with his clairvoyant view of God-in-all, called for "application of the senses" to prayer. His method of meditating requires that we step out of ourselves and into a Gospel scene where we become part of the action.

We hear the waves lapping the shore of the Sea of Tiberias; we smell the fresh-caught fish in Peter's net. Together with the disciples, we approach the charcoal fire where Jesus is preparing breakfast. "Come and eat your meal," he says to them and to us. Like the others, we haven't the nerve to ask, "Is it really you?" We feel in our hearts that it is indeed the risen Lord. So we settle down on the beach to eat our fish and bread, and to feast our eyes on the one who serves us (see Jn 21:1-14).

By following Ignatius' advice, we become increasingly able to pass through the Gospel text into the lived reality of our relationship with Christ. We experience the environment in which Jesus moved, teaching, guiding, healing, .correcting, loving, feeding. We are immersed in meditative prayer.

The author of the *Exercises* advised beginners: "Whoever wants to imitate Christ our Lord in the use of his senses should recommend himself to his Divine Majesty...then, after considering each of the senses, say an Our Father."

Consideration   If we have never attempted a sensual approach to the Gospels, can we admit the possibility that Ignatius may be just the person to aid us in prayer?

How do we respond to the image of Jesus as a sensual person? What does this response tell us about ourselves?

Invocation   Ignatius,
with you as my director,
I won't be able to sit around thinking about prayer.
You are a person of action as well as contemplation,
and you expect me to exercise my spiritual faculties
    faithfully.
Although your method and your pace may intimidate me
    a bit,
I'm ready to give it a try.
Be patient.
And pray that I may give greater glory to God
by my wholehearted immersion in this meditation.
Amen.

Praying With Ignatius: The Upper Room

Meditation   God has gifted you, Ignatius, with great skills as a spiritual director and a tutor in prayer. Entrusting myself to your guidance, I will prepare to follow you into Jerusalem for the Last Supper of our Lord Jesus Christ. I will absorb the details of this feast of love in which Jesus communes with his dearest companions. I will recall how he sent two of his disciples from Bethany to Jerusalem to make preparations for the Passover Supper, the seder of the Jewish people. With you I will join Jesus and the disciples gathered in the Upper Room to share the commemoration of Yahweh's redemption of the Chosen People, seeing how Jesus washed his friends' feet and fed them with his own body and blood. I will watch how Jesus led his friends off to the Mount of Olives while Judas went away to betray him.

Intercede for me, Ignatius, that I may enter fully into the Gospel scene and experience this first Eucharist as though it were unfolding before me. May the Spirit of God give me eyes that see and ears that hear! Direct me, brother-saint, and I will follow.

The Upper Room is large and furnished only with those things necessary for a proper seder. The whitewashed walls are bare and clean; small windows open to the night air. A low table has been set in the middle of the room, surrounded by couches and cushions supplied by the well-to-do host.

Two disciples (the early arrivals) and several women of the household have prepared all the ritual foods and laid them out in their traditional places: a roast lamb slaughtered in the Temple courtyard; haroseth (a pastelike compound of apples, nuts, cinnamon and wine) as a reminder of the days when the Jews were forced to lay bricks for the Egyptians; bitter herbs, greens, and salt water into which the herbs will be dipped; matzos (the unleavened bread prepared in haste by the Jews before their flight from Pharaoh) and earthen cups of red wine.

As the disciples enter, chatting in groups of two or three, they sense the welcoming atmosphere created by a generous host. The carefully-laid table tells them that Jesus' wishes have been carried out and that all is ready for the festive meal. A flickering oil lamp, set on a low bronze stand, casts shadows over the room, concealing the imperfections which daylight might expose. Appetites quicken at the aroma of the paschal lamb, the familiar matzos and the glow of the wine which will soon gladden everyone's heart.

At the end of the informal procession making its way to the table are Peter, John and Jesus. Like the others, they are wearing loose woolen cloaks with the prescribed tassels at the corners. Under their cloaks, they wear the colobrium, a plain tunic sometimes woven without a seam, tied at the waist with a folded length of wool. Their leather sandals are covered with dust and their hair has the tousled look of pilgrims who spend their days on the open road.

Peter and John are talking animatedly, anticipating both the meal and the religious ritual they have loved since childhood. Jesus, his arms around their shoulders, is smiling. But he seems to be thinking of something other than their conversation.

Ignatius, you and I are among the disciples who have already settled themselves around the table. Although we see and hear them, they do not distract us as we observe Jesus entering. He is of medium height and slender build with shoulder-length hair, dark like his eyes. His nose is prominent, his face intelligent, his trim beard parted slightly in the middle. Both his cloak and tunic are of wool, undyed and homespun by his mother. He could not be called handsome. But he is good to look at, and we go on looking, secure in the knowledge that we are not noticed.

He takes his place at the table, waits for the silence of his friends and intones the opening Psalm of the *Hallel,* the Psalms of praise:

> "Praise, you servants of the LORD,
>   praise the name of the LORD.
> Blessed be the name of the LORD
>   both now and forever." (Ps 113:1-2)

His voice conveys a reverence as natural as breathing. It is strong, authentic, totally without pious pretension. He opens the *Haggadah* in which the ancient ceremonial rite is inscribed. Chanting, he prays the *Kiddush:*

> Blessed are you, Lord, our God, King of the Universe,
> who created the fruit of the vine.
> Blessed are you, Lord, our God, King of the Universe,
> who chose us above all peoples,
> and exalted us above all tongues,
> and hallowed us with your commandments.

The blessings follow, one after another, praising God for

the gifts of light, life, bread, wine, freedom from oppression. Thanksgiving overflows the hearts of the guests, filling the room with warmth and purpose. As the meal progresses at a leisurely pace, Jesus often looks into the faces around the table, seeking recognition that this seder will be unlike any other. His friends are attentive but unaware of his urgency.

He rises and removes his cloak. Several disciples, relaxed and leaning back away from the table, go on eating and talking quietly. Jesus picks up a towel, placed near the table for the ceremonial washing of hands, and wraps it around his waist. Then he pours water into a basin and begins washing Thomas' feet. The disciple is startled, but he makes only a mumbled objection, knowing that Jesus often does strange things which he later explains to them.

Without comment, Jesus moves from Thomas to James, drying their feet with a mother's tenderness. Out of respect, no one has questioned him.

When he comes to Peter, objections greet him. "Lord, are you going to wash my feet?" (Jn 13:6). Peter is offended that the one he has identified as the Messiah should bend to this menial task.

Jesus looks up at him, assuring him that the purpose of his actions will soon become clear. But Peter will have none of it. He jerks his feet back under his cloak; his face is masked by embarrassment and confusion. Knowing the heart of his gruff friend, Jesus says, "If I do not wash you, you will have no share in my heritage" (Jn 13:8). And Peter, like a boy who has been scolded by his father, tries to make amends by insisting that Jesus wash his hands and head as well as his dusty feet. You sense the Lord's hidden laughter as he bends to his task, loving Peter's excessive compliance.

When Jesus comes to us, I follow your lead. You swallow shame and false humility, knowing that he does not require worthiness of his friends. The water is cool, his hands gentle, a Mary-touch he well remembers and makes his own. I no longer feel reluctant. Only loved and cared for.

Jesus again reclines at the table. His friends await the explanation that will set them at ease. If he has done something not prescribed in the *Haggadah,* he has a good reason for it.

"Do you understand what I just did for you?" (Jn 13:12)

They are leaning toward him, hoping for an answer not veiled by a parable.

"You address me as 'Teacher' and 'Lord,'
and fittingly enough,
for that is what I am.
But if I washed your feet—
I who am Teacher and Lord—
then you must wash each other's feet.
What I just did was to give you an example:
as I have done, so must you do." (Jn 13:13-15)

He pauses to be sure that they are all with him.

"I solemnly assure you,
no slave is greater than his master;
no messenger outranks the one who sent him.
Once you know all these things,
blest will you be if you put them into practice." (Jn 13:16-17)

The disciples are silent, enjoying again his gift for culling wisdom out of the ordinary. How many times has he opened their eyes during the past three years? How often have they sat together like this, taking pleasure in his presence as teacher and friend? They haven't always understood him. But they have come a long way since he first called them out of darkness into his own light.

Jesus' face is suffused with emotion. He gathers them all in with his glance as he says, "I have greatly desired to eat this Passover with you before I suffer. I tell you, I will not eat again until it is fulfilled in the kingdom of God" (Lk 22:15-16).

The disciples look to each other in apprehension at his change in mood, the unsettling tremor in his voice. They have seen him weep before. But this is something deeper than tears. Minutes pass. The lamplight flickers erratically. Gravity enters, an uninvited guest.

Jesus takes a cup of wine, offers a blessing and says: "Take this and divide it among you; I tell you, from now on I will not drink of the fruit of the vine until the coming of the reign of God" (Lk 22:17-18). He raises the cup, holding it out toward his friends.

Then Jesus takes bread, gives thanks, breaks the bread and shares it with them, saying, "This is my body to be given for you. Do this as a remembrance of me" (Lk 22:19). Solemnly, like men in a dream, each of the disciples takes a broken piece of matzo and eats it. No one questions Jesus. He seems to have passed into another world, taking them with him.

Then he takes the cup of wine and hands it to them, saying: "This cup is the new covenant in my blood, which will be shed for you" (Lk 22:20). John drinks from the cup and passes it to James as the others wait, lost in their private reflections on the meaning of what they are about to do.

Jesus has become the new Paschal Lamb, giving his flesh and blood for the lives of those he loves. He is the Bread of Life who satisfies all hunger, the Wine of Life who quenches all thirst. For this mystical interlude around the table, his disciples accept and believe. They are one.

In this shadowed room where unleashed faith makes all things possible, we feel the bond of love by which Jesus has drawn his friends to him. We are raised up by the beauty of this night in which a new covenant has been realized. We are held by the stillness in which the Word of God has spoken.

When the Body and Blood of Christ come to us, we receive him hungrily and he ignites in our hearts the fire he has come on earth to start. We look into his face and see the anguish of a love that can never be satisfied until it is poured out, like choice wine, to the last drop.

While in communion with Jesus, we ask him to allow us to enter into his experience of this night. Feel the grief and helplessness he has taken on himself for our sake. Recognize the love that willingly suffers for us. Feel sorrow for our past refusals to respond to that love. You look at Jesus. You stay with him. And so do I.

I ask myself: What can I do for Jesus who is prepared to go to his death for me?

At your direction, Ignatius, I will let this question consume whatever time it requires. There is no other reality at this moment than the Upper Room, the Last Supper, the loving host who awaits my answer.

After a while, Jesus stirs himself from the reverie that has enveloped everyone at the table. Lifting the fourth and final cup of blessing, he prays: "Blessed are you, Lord, our God, King of the Universe, who created the fruit of the vine." The disciples drain their cups. Jesus returns to the *Haggadah*:

> O, may he who is most mighty soon rebuild his house;
> speedily, speedily, soon, in our days;
> O God, rebuild it, O Eternal, rebuild it,
> rebuild your house in good time.

When the *Haggadah* has been completed, the disciples pull their cloaks about them and rise to sing the concluding Psalms. The joy of the supper has become a sorrow they do not yet understand and are not yet willing to deal with. Jesus lifts his arms to the Father and begins:

> Give thanks to the LORD, for he is good,
>   for his mercy endures forever.
> Let the house of Israel say,
>   "His mercy endures forever." (Ps 118:1-2)

As the chant continues, Jesus leads the procession toward the door. He seeks the company of his Father on the Mount of Olives. The male voices—rough, earnest, intensified by the wine and loosed emotion—gradually dim as the disciples leave the house and follow Jesus up the road. I stay behind with you and pray as Jesus taught us: "Our Father…"

Reflection   The *Spiritual Exercises* of St. Ignatius provide a pattern of
prayer that can involve me in the central events of
Christ's life on earth. The pattern will remain meaningless unless
I am willing to liberate my senses in a meditation that goes
beyond "thinking about" to "being there."

Can I pray in this Ignatian manner? Why or why not?

Has the Last Supper meditation revealed anything to me
about Jesus? About myself? About prayer?

Praying Like Ignatius:
A Parish Celebration of the Eucharist

Meditation   O Lord my God,
King of the Universe and Lord of my life,
I come to you with a desire to be a more eucharistic
   person,
a person dedicated to thankfulness for the gift of your
   Son,
the bounteous gift of his Body and Blood
which I have, until now, failed to appreciate as I might.
Let your Spirit imprint on my heart
images of the Last Supper
so that I may never tire of reflecting
on what happened in that Upper Room.
May I realize more clearly with each Eucharist
that Jesus gives himself to me in bread and wine,
and that I must give myself in memory of him.
I ask this in Jesus' name. Amen.

"I solemnly assure you,

it was not Moses who gave you bread from the heavens;
it is my Father who gives you the real heavenly bread.
God's bread comes down from heaven
and gives life to the world....
I myself am the bread of life.
No one who comes to me shall ever be hungry,
no one who believes in me shall ever thirst." (Jn 6:32-33, 35)

In my imagination, I place myself in my parish church on Sunday morning. I see the altar, the tabernacle, the sanctuary lamp, the lectern and the candles, the statues and the stained glass windows, the stations of the cross. Although I have often come into this sacred place thoughtlessly or reluctantly, today I come with gratitude and attention.

I hear the rhythm of the church doors swinging as the worshipers arrive: children with quick, unceremonious stride; elderly people with slow, shuffling tread; teenagers lagging behind purposeful parents; the murmuring of large families settling themselves like flocks of birds; the unobtrusive entrance of single people who slide into side pews as though they were arriving without an invitation.

Seemingly unrelated and often ignoring each other, they are the Body of Christ, present in this church. Blind to their own reality, they see Jesus only in the bread. But whether they know it or not, they form the Body that exists to worship the Father.

"Yet an hour is coming, and is already here,
when authentic worshipers
will worship the Father in Spirit and truth.
Indeed, it is just such worshipers
the Father seeks.
God is Spirit,
and those who worship him
must worship in Spirit and truth." (Jn 4:23-24)

Aware of myself as a member of the Body of Christ, as a worshiper in Spirit and truth, I resolve to attend to this liturgy. I will focus my senses on this prayer of the universal Church, this prayer that is the heart of all action and contemplation, this prayer which is Jesus raised up and returned to us.

As the entrance song begins, I remember the disciples singing the first Psalm of the *Hallel:*

> Praise, you servants of the LORD,
>   praise the name of the LORD. (Ps 113:1)

I sing for Yahweh as his people have done for centuries. I greet him with a grateful heart because I am free and willing and able to praise him. I hear worship in the voices around me, devotion in the hearts that are, however imperceptibly, lifted up to the Father. Praise Yahweh!

In the Penitential Rite, I remember my sorrow for breaking faith with Jesus. I recall his anguish on the eve of his crucifixion, and praise him for the mercy he never withholds from me:

> You were sent to heal the contrite:
> Lord, have mercy.

> You came to call sinners:
> Christ, have mercy.

> You plead for us at the right hand of the Father:
> Lord, have mercy.

Before praying the Glory to God, I take St. Ignatius' motto as my own. I begin now to do all "for the greater glory of God." The words of this beautiful hymn come not from my head, but from my center. I am carried along by its billowing adoration:

> For you alone are the Holy One,
> you alone are the Lord,
> you alone are the Most High,
>   Jesus Christ,
>   with the Holy Spirit,
>   in the glory of God the Father.

I prepare to receive the Word by making some sign of

reverence toward the Bible (or the Lectionary) as the sacred story book of God and his people. Through his messenger, the lector, God is about to speak to me in a personal way. I recognize his eagerness to communicate with me and to loose the power of his Word. With regret for all the times I have been deaf to the readings, I listen to them as though my life depended on it. I ruminate on the message with the patience of a lamb chewing its cud, nourished by it.

Feeling the rhythm and emotional color of the Responsorial Psalm, I identify with the psalmist. I am one with all Christians and Jews who have prayed this song for centuries and with all who will be praying it forever. I pray with King David and Solomon, Esther and Ruth, Mary and Joseph, with Christ concealed in the hearts of those around me. This song from the City of God will lead me home.

As I stand for the Gospel, I remember how the great crowds once gathered along the shore of the Sea of Galilee, pressing forward to hear the rabbi from Nazareth. While he sat in a boat where all could see him, Jesus cast out a net of parables and caught their imaginations with a sower, a mustard seed, a pearl of great price. He broke open the mysteries of God's reign and appeased their appetite with truth. But he also warned them not to keep their treasure buried in the back yard: "Let everyone heed what he hears!" (Mt 13:43).

I pray that the treasure of the Gospel, extended through the homily, will be recognized and assimilated, shared and passed on. I call on the Spirit to brood over this body of Christ which has been fed by the Word. With Jeremiah I assure Yahweh:

> When I found your words, I devoured them;
> they became my joy and the happiness of my heart.
>
> (Jer 15:16)

Now the pace of the liturgy is picking up, rising toward the climatic Eucharistic Prayer. I enter into the procession with the gifts, moving in harmony with the expectant chant, "Come, Lord Jesus, come!" I hold in my hands the gifts of prayer, sacrifice and service which, woven together, clothe me in Christ-likeness and draw the Father's blessings upon me.

I watch the choreography of celebrant and servers as the table is set for the Eucharistic meal, remembering the table in the Upper Room, the festive spirit of the seder. I enter into the continuity of the Consecration: "Do this in memory of me." I see again the four eucharistic actions: he took, blessed, broke, gave. Here before me is the Body that was broken, the Blood that was poured out. All around me is the Body made up of many members, each called by Baptism to drink of the Spirit and eat of the Lord.

Just as I need Christ in the Eucharist, I need Christ in his Mystical Body. To recognize one and not the other is to remain blind in one eye. I feel my kinship with those beside me, before me, behind me. When I pray the Our Father I make their intentions, their sufferings and their joys my own. I ask to be reconciled with any who may have offended me, and try to judge no one because all are members of Christ.

At the Communion Rite, I remember the communal atmosphere of the Last Supper. It was not a private tête-à-tête between Jesus and Peter or Jesus and John. It was a fellowship meal in which Jesus gave himself to his friends and expected them to do the same for others. I look into the faces of men, women and children who have been fed by the Eucharistic Lord. Touched by their faith, their hopes, their struggle to remain Christian in a secular society, I pray that each member may become one with him who has, as St. John Chrysostom said, "kneaded his body with ours."

During the Concluding Rite, I hear the disciples singing the *Hallel* with Jesus before he goes out into the night to wrestle with obedience:

> I will give thanks to you, for you have answered me
>   and have been my savior....
> You are my God, and I give thanks to you;
>   O my God, I extol you.
> Give thanks to the LORD, for he is good;

for his kindness endures forever. (Ps 118:21, 28-29)

Before leaving the church, I speak to Jesus of what I will do today in memory of him.

Reflection   It's easy to be an unsensual Christian at a Sunday liturgy. We can be physically present, emotionally absent and spiritually vacant with no trouble at all. If we are stimulated neither by the music nor the celebrant, our senses lie like old dogs by the fireside. We rarely think of rousing them as we follow the familiar rites.

How can I pray the liturgy with greater awareness and sense involvement?

How can I awaken my senses to the taken-for-granted elements of every liturgy:
—the physical proximity of other persons;
—the merging of voices in prayer and song;
—the play of light through stained glass windows;
—the designs and fabrics of vestments;
—the smell of incense and burning candles;
—the symbolism of standing, kneeling and sitting at
    prayer;
—the domestic movements of the celebrant as he
    prepares the table;
—the connections established by the sign of peace;
—the breaking and eating of bread;
—the tasting and drinking of wine;
—the communion procession of the Body of Christ;
—the messages conveyed by folded hands, bowed heads,
    attentive listeners?

Am I a eucharistic person who can pray with Dag Hammarskjold, "For all that has been, thanks; to all that shall be, yes!"?

Exploring Further

Response   The preceding meditations on the Last Supper and a
parish liturgy are adaptations of the Ignatian approach to
meditation. They are aperitifs preceding the four-course meal of
the *Spiritual Exercises*. Whoever would learn the way of Ignatius
must consult the Jesuit founder himself—through a retreat or a
spiritual director experienced in the *Exercises*.

Contemporary versions of the saint's classic work (see
p. 80) free us from the hassles of having to decipher Ignatius'
convoluted and anachronistic style. They retain the spirit and
pattern while adapting the language to our time. By helping us
apply memory, understanding and will to the Gospels, they
enable us to move inside the mysteries we have contemplated
from the surface.

Although the *Exercises* are not for everyone, they provide
good counsel for anyone who wants to advance in prayer. They
remind us of the intrinsic relationship between prayer and self-
examination, for how can we grow in prayer if we are not
maturing in holiness? Ignatius insists on a regular examination of
conscience in which we face up to our sinfulness and seek daily
forgiveness so that we can do better tomorrow. In this way, we
can never forget our spiritual poverty and radical dependence on
God.

As a practical matter, the examen gives us a sense of
having done something definite, of moving forward toward the
person we intend to be. By focusing our energies on improving
particular points, we are more apt to let the Spirit put our house
in order.

The *Exercises* also reveal the wisdom of reconsidering
certain passages of Scripture that glimmer for us like polished
stones. By meditating affectively on a parable or a Psalm again
and again, we work it deeper into our consciousness where it
informs our actions and feeds our prayer. We come to know it
and live it by heart.

Our response to the prayer-way of Ignatius may be as complex as undertaking the complete *Spiritual Exercises* or as simple as a sensual consideration of a single Gospel scene. The following Jesus-events lend themselves readily to an Ignatian meditation:

> Jesus feeds 5,000 people...Mt 14:13-21
> Jesus heals a paralytic...Mk 2:1-12
> Jesus is rejected by his hometown...Lk 4:14-30
> Jesus and the penitent woman...Lk 7:36-50
> Jesus hosts a picnic...Jn 21:1-14
> Jesus teaches Peter the meaning of love...Jn 21:15-19

Another Ignatian way to fortify our prayer is to take a creative approach to penance. Few of us have the stamina to subsist on the old bread-and-water regime. But we are all capable of less dramatic means which achieve the desired result without feeding our pride or calling attention to our saintliness: passing up a favorite dessert or a drink before dinner; planning a weekly Third World meal; cutting back on coffee or tea; accepting without comment foods we abhor; giving up snacks; leaving the table before we are full.

Perhaps the best response to Ignatius' example would be to make room in our lives for an annual retreat—a weekend or longer devoted entirely to our spiritual health. The invitation comes first from Jesus: "Come by yourselves to an out-of-the-way place and rest a little" (Mk 6:31).

Also consider the possibility of finding a spiritual director who can set you on the right path to prayer and guide your progress. As well as priests and religious, there are many laypersons trained and gifted in this ministry. A good director will listen well, advise sparingly, challenge wisely and pray unerringly for your spiritual growth.

Finally, as a sensual Christian, take delight in this

message from the prologue of John's First Epistle:

> This is what we proclaim to you:
> what was from the beginning,
> what we have heard,
> what we have seen with our eyes,
> what we have looked upon
> and our hands have touched—
> we speak of the word of life. (1 Jn 1:1)

Reading   Grow more familiar with Ignatius and his *Exercises* in
these books:

The Ignatian Way to God, by Alexandre Brou and translated by
William J. Young (Milwaukee: Bruce Publishing, 1952).

Ignatius the Theologian, by Hugo Rahner (New York: Herder &
Herder, 1968).

A Living Room Retreat, by Sister Helen Cecilia Swift, S.N.D.
de N. (Cincinnati: St. Anthony Messenger Press, 1981).
Accompanying taped direction is also available.

Saints for All Seasons, edited by John J. Delaney (Garden City:
Doubleday, 19787).

St. Ignatius of Loyola, by Giorgio Papasogli and translated by Paul
Garvin (New York: Society of St. Paul, 1959).

St. Ignatius' Own Story, by Ignatius Loyola as told to Luis
Gonzalez de Camara; translated by William J. Young (New
York: Henry Regnery, 1956).

*The Spiritual Exercises of St. Ignatius: A Literal Translation and a
Contemporary Reading,* by David L. Fleming (St. Louis: The
Institute of Jesuit Sources, 1978).

THERESE
OF LISIEUX
1873-1897

The Woman Warrior

Getting to Know Therese

Life-Sketch   Therese of Lisieux was as militaristic as Joan of Arc and as nonviolent as Dorothy Day. She loved a good fight, but the battleground had to be interior. Those who know her only as the Little Flower, a Victorian rose blooming sweetly in a cloister garden, will have trouble recognizing her as the fierce campaigner who wrote: "Let us fight without ceasing, even without hope of winning the battle. What does success matter! Let us keep going, however exhausting the struggle may be."

Her campaigns were fought against the powers of darkness, those forces of self-will which occupy the territory between our false and true selves. She was fearless in spiritual warfare, retreating only when she could not defeat the enemy by an act of charity.

From the time she entered the Carmel of Lisieux at 15, Therese armed herself with prayer and sacrifice for the struggle against hypocrisy, indulgence, pride, laxity, intolerance and possessiveness. Love was, to her, more a war cry than sentimental affection. "God wanted to make me conquer the fortress of Carmel at sword's point," she said. That sword of the Spirit was the Word of God.

Her military strategist was the luminous Carmelite, St. John of the Cross. She translated his complex doctrine of detachment into a deceptively simple path to sanctity which she called "the Little Way." We are inclined to picture Therese making her way to heaven by picking up dropped pins and cheerfully scrubbing dirty laundry. But there was a bit more to the Little Way than that.

To keep to the Way, she had to practice a humility as powerful as Martin Luther King's courage. Day after trying day, she welcomed unjust criticism, asked for the menial jobs no one else wanted, befriended those who most annoyed her, helped those who returned no gratitude, endured the cloister's stinging cold without complaint, shared her time and her inspired ideas as though they belonged to all, and bore pain and physical incapacity as gracefully as others bear good fortune.

She lived a common life in uncommon awareness that every act done out of love is valued by God. These "trifles," she dared to say, pleased Jesus more than great deeds of recognized holiness. Her way was frightening in its scope and consoling in its availability to every person of goodwill.

In Therese's best-selling autobiography, *The Story of a Soul*, we can all see our better selves. She exemplifies the countless invisible victories of daily life, the unheralded conquests over selfishness which we too can claim: smiling service to a nagging invalid, attention willingly paid to a silly bore, possessions given away without thought of a return, time shared freely, acceptance of unearned blame, suffering hidden under a peaceful exterior.

We find in Therese the full blooming of our own potential for unselfish action, our natural inclination toward sanctity. She is the good Christian we'd like to be—if we just had the time and patience to pay attention to the minor challenges that confront us daily in the disguise of the ordinary. If we take Therese seriously, we can not deny that holiness is within our grasp.

Her life was short, but she wasted none of it. At an age when most young ladies were taken up with flirtations and fancy wardrobes, Therese was beseiging religious authorities—including the Pope himself—to allow her early entrance into Carmel. She dedicated herself to the Little Way and followed it ever deeper into the dark regions of self-annihilation.

Therese died in an agony of suffocation caused by advanced tuberculosis when she was 24. For a year and a half she had suffered hemorrhages, coughing spells, fevers and debilitating weakness. She had prayed for a martyrdom of body and soul; she received both. Her physical decline was matched by a withering of spiritual health. Bombarded by temptations against faith, she lost for the first time her vital intuition of heaven.

The woman warrior shielded herself with the gospel, observing, "To be really brave means asking for the cross when one's heart is full of fear, and withstanding this fear like Our Lord in the Garden of Olives."

Portrait   No less likely candidate for military glory could be found than the charming and pampered little Therese Martin, last of five daughters born to Louis and Zelie Martin in the provincial French town of Alençon. She enjoyed all the middle-class pleasures of seaside holidays, family festivities and assorted pets. She was as sheltered as a figurine in a glass menagerie.

Her childhood photographs reflect a self-possessed personality softened by blonde tendrils and lace collars. Therese looks every inch the proper young lady, the feminine persona on a pedestal. Her family adored her. Happily, they expressed their love by giving Therese all the advantages that mattered: a home permeated by vibrant Catholicism, a taste for virtue, an introduction to prayer and a desire to serve God.

Unlike many of us who are drawn to meditation in childhood and later lose the knack of it, Therese nourished her attraction to silent prayer, which she termed "dreaming of heaven." When she went fishing with her father, she often put down her line and sat contemplating nature, contrasting the world which passes with the paradise of her imagination. She had a curtained-off cubbyhole behind her bed where she could be alone with her thoughts of God. Even then she recognized that it was "better to speak to God than about him." Why? Because our spiritual discussions are often sullied with self-love.

Therese's older sister Pauline, later her superior at Carmel, tutored her in the ways of prayer and self-conquest; this was her basic training in the art of spiritual warfare. By the time she entered the convent, she was ready to meet the gospel challenge. Like Francis of Assisi, Therese was never satisfied with half-measures. She wanted to be a saint and she took the straightest path she could find.

Her autobiography provides ample proof that Therese was a warrior of admirable mettle. One typical example: An uneducated and rather conceited Sister managed to irritate Therese in everything she did. Instead of avoiding her, Therese took the Little Way straight into the fray: "And I set myself to treat her as if I loved her best of all." She was so successful that, after Therese's death, this same Sister could say, "During her life, I made her really happy."

Summarizing her religious life, Sister Therese of the Child Jesus observed: "All I did was to break my self-will, check a hasty reply, and do little kindnesses without making a fuss about them."

That's all she did. And she did it so well that one of her companions felt obliged to comment, while Therese was on her deathbed, "She's never done anything worth talking about." The fallen warrior must have taken that as the highest compliment.

Prayer-Life   If Therese had tried the *Spiritual Exercises* of Ignatius, she might have wound up with a migraine. Structured approaches to prayer confused and dissatisfied her. In self-defense she limited her reading to the Bible and the works of John of the Cross. Prayer, for Therese, was a matter of being herself: "I just say what I want to say to God quite simply and he never fails to understand."

When she felt isolated from God or lethargic about praying, Therese slowly prayed an Our Father and a Hail Mary, savoring the words as though they were a delicacy prepared for a patient with no appetite. She tried to get down into these familiar prayers, finding their mystical meanings.

Spiritual dryness was as well-known to Therese as it is to most of us. But she buckled down and forced herself to act as if she were enjoying the consolations of the inspired. She was wise enough to know that the purpose of prayer is not to satisfy ourselves, but to please God. She was strong enough to say, "In all my relations with Jesus, I feel nothing," and keep right on praying.

Therese brought the attitudes of confidence and familiarity to her prayer. Because her awareness of God's love had been tended in early childhood, she could easily relate to the Father as her loving Papa and to Jesus as her beloved. Through her family's example, she had come to realize that the Lord is "more tender than a mother" and, knowing this, she did not need constant reassurances of his love.

She devised an ingenuous image to call to mind whenever prayer seemed to be a futile exercise in talking to herself. Therese pictured Jesus asleep in her boat as he once slept in Peter's vessel. But she did not awaken him—even when the storms of doubt or suffering threatened her. She knew he was there, taking advantage of the rest she offered. That was enough.

Unlike most saints, Therese frankly tells us that she experienced few consolations in prayer. She was not carried away by beautiful visions or awed by celestial voices. After receiving the Eucharist, she sometimes fell asleep. The Lord remained silent when she most wanted to hear from him. As she wryly comments in *The Story of a Soul*, "He does not trouble himself to make conversation."

For her part, Therese does not trouble herself about past failures or future concerns. Sufficient to the day are the skirmishes thereof. She understands the significance of the present moment as an opportunity to act lovingly. In her poem "The Eternal Today" (*L'Eternel Aujourd'hui*), she says:

> My life is an instant,
> An hour which passes by;
> My life is a moment
> Which I have no power to stay.
> You know, O my God,
> That to love you here on earth—
> I have only today.

Letting Therese Teach Us

Approach Therese took a straight-arrow approach to prayer. She always aimed right at the heart of the matter. No image fits her better than the one she gave herself, the woman warrior brandishing the sword of the Spirit. In prayer she aggressively asked, "Lord, God of Hosts, who has said to us in the Gospel, 'I have come not to bring peace, but the sword,' arm me for the struggle." Sanctity, as surely as Macbeth's castle, could be won at sword's point, and Therese wasn't afraid to use her two-edged weapon.

She thought of herself as a soldier who treats the wounds of others with seriousness and compassion, but her own as mere scratches. When the enemy appeared to have the upper hand, Therese met difficulties either by going under them (like a G.I. negotiating a barbed-wire fence), or by retreating without a single volley. In this way she survived to fight another day.

During her last illness, Therese remained on the front lines and rallied others who were tempted to give up on the battle against selfishness. She wrote to Sister Marie of St. Joseph, exhorting her to respond to provocation not with stones but with charity for the sake of the "Great General" under whose command the Carmelites served. She asked, with characteristic valor, "Grapeshot, the roar of cannon, what is any of it when one is upheld by the General?"

nsideration Can we gain confidence in our prayer by reflecting on Therese's straightforward approach?

How does her experience as a person who persisted in prayer without consolation or assurance touch us?

Can her view of the spiritual life as a campaign against self-will have any application to our life?

Therese,
valiant woman warrior,
train me in spiritual combat.
Let me see you within the walls of your fortress,
routing anger at annoyances,
felling desires for self-justification,
stopping irritation in its tracks.
Enlist my willingness to learn your Little Way,
the way of the foot soldier who receives no silver medals.
With you, I pray:

Blessed be the LORD, my rock,
    who trains my hands for battle, my fingers for war;
My refuge and my fortress,
    my stronghold, my deliverer,
My shield in whom I trust.... (Ps 144:1-2)

Praying With Therese: Carmel of Lisieux

Meditation The Carmelite convent which is your home, Therese,
reflects the severity and simplicity of the lives it harbors.
Bare brick and stone, plain wood and uncurtained glass greet
your eyes with consistent refusal to provide distraction. You have
foresworn Victorian embellishment for gospel clarity, cultivating
beauty within. Robed in brown wool, you are yet a white-veiled
novice seeking ways to prove yourself as a candidate for Christ's
service. It is winter and the unheated cloister tests your resolve
with rigid cold.

    In your heart simmers the lesson of the Good Samaritan.
Who are the wounded travelers along your narrow road? What
solace do you have to offer? The answers rise to the surface where
meditation prompts action. Among your sisters in the
community, there is one from whom you shrink with fear. Sister

St. Peter is an elderly professed nun firmly rooted in her accustomed ways. Her ill-health is matched by ill-temper that vents itself in dissatisfaction whenever things are not done just so.

Every day precisely at 5:50 p.m. Sister St. Peter leaves the chapel in the midst of early evening prayers to make her awkward way down the cloister passageway to the refectory, where she must be suitably settled in at the supper table before the rest of the community arrives. She has not asked for help, but her pace and pained expressions are an appeal that the Samaritan cannot ignore. Your reluctance to volunteer is defeated by determination to offer her "a feast of cheerful charity."

Like a warrior donning protective armor, you sheath yourself in preparatory prayer:

> O Most High, when I begin to fear,
>   in you will I trust.
>   In God, in whose promise I glory,
>   in God I trust without fear;
>   what can flesh do against me? (Ps 56:4)

If Sister St. Peter remains impossible to please, so much the better. She will be a worthy challenge to you.

Testing-time arrives. While you are chanting a favorite Psalm, you see Sister St. Peter impatiently shaking her hourglass and putting aside her breviary. That is the signal. Fasten on the buckler of patience and humility. Go to her as eagerly as if she were the Lord Jesus himself waiting for you to take his arm.

In harsh whispers that disturb the community, the commands are issued, rat-a-tat, pricking your sensitivity: "Pick up the stool with both hands. Be careful, don't hit the bench with it! Carry it with your left hand, Sister—can't you see you need your right hand to guide me? Don't make such a commotion! For heaven's sake, get off my heel! Can't you watch where you're going?"

You are out in the passageway, away from the music of the Office and the warmth of the sanctuary lamp. Hanging on to the back of your companion's belt, you attempt to secure her progress among the shadows while making yourself inconspicuous. Again the artillery is loosed, this time in strident voice unfettered by the decorum of the chapel:

"You're going too fast. Are you trying to push me over, Sister? I knew you were too young to look after me properly. Why did I consent to this? I can't imagine why you volunteered to help if you can't do any better at it than this. I never had this much trouble when I came by myself!"

At last you reach the refectory, the high ground, the promise of relief. But Sister St. Peter's fretful journey encompasses yet more difficulties. She must be settled carefully and correctly at the table in her assigned place. "Put the stool right here—not too close to the table. This isn't right! Push it in just a little at a time. My sleeves must be turned back. Keep them flat, Sister. Watch what you're doing! I can see you have much to learn."

She expects you to leave now. You are free to depart from the front line, to get out of the range of her displeasure. But she is fumbling with her bread, trying to slice it into equal sections, and the knife trembles in her arthritic hand. You offer to help, flinching under the renewed volley of instructions and warnings. Then you smile at her, letting the smile arise from deep below the surface provinces of dislike and irritation.

The verbal battering has tired you as thoroughly as an afternoon of window-washing. You wonder if you will be able to enter the fray day after day, hearing the same complaints, bearing the same insults, performing the same trivial tasks, missing the tonic of community prayer. Will you be able to keep the smile on your mouth, relishing compliance? Or will you lash her with accusations of ingratitude?

You turn to prayer quickly before courage crumbles into righteousness:

O LORD, set a watch before my mouth,
a guard at the door of my lips. (Ps 141:3)

Reflection   If I am tempted to think that Therese's volunteering to
help Sister St. Peter was an insignificant victory, I will
pause to consider how many times I have ignored, backed away
from or refused to take up similar challenges to charity.

I think of several people who irritate me, who bore me or
who dislike me. When was the last time I invited such a
person to dinner, offered to help with a difficult project,
listened to the person without being defensive?

I think of one person who is hard to get along with. What
am I willing to do for this person out of love for Jesus,
who cherishes him or her?

Praying Like Therese: Into the Fray

Meditation   Lord Jesus,
like my sister-saint Therese,
I want to make your Word my weapon
against the forces that separate me from my better self.
Let me see my everyday relationships
in the light of your truth,
so that I will know where the battle lies.
Enlist me in your service.
Command me in your charity.
Rally me with the forceful presence of your Spirit.
Amen, Jesus, Amen.

I place myself in a setting (at home, at work, at school, in
a hospital or nursing home) where I often encounter a person

who challenges my readiness to be charitable. It may be someone close to me (a husband or wife, son or daughter, mother or father) who always brings out the worst in me.

Perhaps he or she has what I consider an unbearable prejudice, a way of needling me, a habit of making unreasonable requests, a bent for embarrassing me in front of others, a disregard for my privacy or free time.

It may be a sick or handicapped relative who constantly speaks self-pity, who expects too much of me and rarely expresses any thanks for my thoughtfulness, who drives me to distraction with eccentric or annoying behavior.

It may be a neighbor or an acquaintance whose close friendship I have avoided because the person is unintelligent or insensitive, pushy, dishonest or disliked by others, offensive or seemingly inferior to me.

It may be an employer or co-worker who puts me down, takes credit for my ideas or shows little appreciation for my efforts, who is hypocritical in his or her relationship with me or impossible to please.

I envision a particular situation in which this person offends or irritates me by his or her actions, attitudes, complaints or requests. What is my usual response? Do I resort to anger? Defensive tactics? Excuses? Noninvolvement? Impatience? Criticism? Repugnance?

Now I envision what my response might be if, at the moment of a difficult encounter, I could arm myself with the Word of God, in the manner of Therese. I hear Jesus telling me, "N._____, whatever you do to _____, you do to me" (see Mt 25:40).

I hear Jesus' words in a new way because they are addressed directly to me. Jesus literally means that if I insult or ignore this person, I am doing so to him. There is no other interpretation which will allow me a way out.

The enemies of my better self insistently remind me that this person does not deserve to be treated charitably. This person will not appreciate my kindness. He will go right on being

94

difficult; she will deride me or take advantage of my goodwill.

They urge me to protect myself against any invasions into my peace of mind, my sense of security, my private space. They insinuate that I will be stepped on or made a fool of. But I hear the whining selfishness in these voices and recognize them as enemies.

I see myself responding to the person with love, patience and humor, with assistance, humility and acceptance. I enjoy the feeling that I have, in this one everyday encounter, emerged victorious. I feel the strength that comes from overpowering my negative impulses.

> You indeed, O LORD, give light to my lamp;
>> O my God, you brighten the darkness about me;
> For with your aid I run against an armed band,
>> and by the help of my God I leap over a wall. (Ps 18:29-30)

Reflection Therese drew her inspiration for prayerful action from the Gospels, which she never tired of considering. As I reflect on my relationship with a person who tests my ability to be charitable, I allow my spirit to ponder one of the sayings of Jesus which apply most directly to me:

> "Blest are the lowly; they shall inherit the land." (Mt 5:5)

> "Blest are they who show mercy; mercy shall be theirs."
>> (Mt 5:7)

> "If you love those who love you, what merit is there in that?"
>> (Mt 5:46)

> "Whoever does the will of my heavenly Father is brother and sister and mother to me." (Mt 12:50)

> "The king will answer them: 'I assure you, as often as you did it for one of my least brothers, you did it for me.'" (Mt 25:45)

I mull over my chosen saying until I see how it can become a sword of the Spirit for me.

Praying With Therese:
Victory at Carmel

Meditation   You look out at chestnut trees bereft of leaves, Therese,
and the cold roams freely about the cloister. Only the
community room is blessed with a fire. Once warmed, you must
walk (no running, no clasping your broad sleeves) down the open
passageway to your cell. You suffer from the contrast and wish
you had not stood before the fire. Now the wind seems to be
attacking the marrow of your bones.

Soon it will be time for your daily encounter with Sister
St. Peter. Her acceptance has been hard-won. She still finds you
an imperfect guide, but she occasionally acknowledges your
smile. The past year has added new burdens of frailty which
undermine her efforts to be more congenial.

The little battles come closer together now as you become
a more seasoned warrior. In the winter darkness of your cell, you
call on the Lord for strength and fortitude: "Lord, all my strength
lies in prayer and sacrifice. They are my invincible weapons, and
I know by experience that they can soften the heart much better
than words. Arm me once again that I may serve you with
greater love today."

You are grateful for the conquests Jesus has already
granted:

Sister X., who is insensitive and tiresome, enjoys all the
attention you have given her at the recreation hour.

Sister M. has multiplied your store of patience by
regularly splashing grimy wash water in your face as she scrubs
the handkerchiefs. Now you seek out this "novel kind of
aspersion" every wash day as a refresher for your humility.

Sister A., who habitually fidgets with her rosary or
breviary pages during meditation in the chapel, has given you an
opportunity to listen as attentively to her agitating noises as you
would to a soothing sonata.

Each conquest enables you to burrow deeper into the

meaning of "whatsoever you do...."

When you see Sister St. Peter shaking her hourglass, you no longer feel reluctance. The prayer you are about to offer is more forceful than the pleasant words you would enjoy reciting in chapel.

The Lord himself said he came not to bring peace, but the sword. There is a time for peace and a time for whacking the enemies of selflessness. The Kingdom is gained by routing complacency, superiority and pride.

In the dark hall, Sister St. Peter shuffles painfully along her appointed route, muttering against the cold and your too-sprightly pace. Then, above the wind and the grumbling of your companion, you imagine you hear distant orchestral music, a sound as foreign to this place as the commotion of Paris traffic. The music evokes a mental picture of a richly-furnished drawing room burnished by chandelier and firelight. In it several young women of fashion are poised on velvet settees like brittle mannequins. They are exchanging empty compliments, pretending to admire what they envy or despise.

Their cultured voices are in jarring counterpoint to the high-pitched complaints of poor Sister St. Peter, who seems unable to find anything right with the world. You turn away from the glowing image to contemplate the cloister's bare walls, the wooden floor worn by the daily passing of sandals, the unlit passageway before you. Instantly, you see it all washed with the light of truth. Gratitude stands firmly against the cold. You know that you would never exchange the 10 minutes of this present act of charity for a thousand years of meaningless pleasures.

You recognize the presence of the Lord and cover Sister St. Peter's chilled hand with your own. From your storehouse of prayer, the psalmist intones:

> ...In the shadow of your wings I shout for joy.
> My soul clings fast to you;
> your right hand upholds me. (Ps 63:8-9)

Reflection The experience of truth, which reaffirmed Therese in spiritual warfare and remained with her like "a fragrant breath from heaven," came only after she had made such acts of charity her daily bread. It seemed to be Jesus' way of saying, "You are fighting the good fight. Remain strong in my love."

I reflect on my relationship with one difficult person. Have my feelings, attitudes, actions in regard to this person been, in any sense, prayerful?

How does my response to this person compare with Therese's response to Sister L., who passed off Therese's inspired thoughts as though they were her own? When Sister L. was praised for her piety and creativity, Therese remained silent, convinced that ideas are gifts from the Spirit, intended to be shared.

How does Jesus view my relationship with this person? What does he expect of me?

Praying Like Therese: Winning the Battle

Meditation Lord,
you know how easy it is for me
to fall prey to old habits
that have sunk their teeth deep into my subconscious.
Unthinking, I react to
insult with anger,
irritation with impatience,
helplessness with disdain,
provocation with a curse.
My enemies gloat over me.
I am like a soldier

who goes into battle armed with straws.
Without prayer and sacrifice,
I cannot be true to your Word or to my self.
Come, free me from falsity.

"He who seeks only himself brings himself to ruin,
whereas he who brings himself to nought for me
discovers who he is." (Mt. 10:39)

I place myself in the cloister garden of Carmel during the
final illness of Sister Therese of the Child Jesus. From her I hope
to learn the secret of wielding charity like a sword in the
campaign of ordinary living. She has already won the battle by
"bringing herself to nought," by becoming so small that her
companions wonder at how little she has accomplished. "Has
ever a soul apparently been less tried than mine?" she asks,
pleased that she can claim no great public victories or heroic
deeds.

What do I see in this emaciated young woman whose
head is supported by pillows and whose hands are too weak for
any task beyond holding a miniature crucifix? I see a soldier-saint
who did absolutely nothing that I cannot do if I take up the same
weapons and use them courageously. I see a woman warrior who
took Jesus at his word and lived by the sword.

Therese wants me to understand the simple demands of
love by which I pray in action. "True charity consists in putting
up with all one's neighbor's faults, never being surprised by his
weakness, and being inspired by the least of his virtues," she says.

None of these challenges can be met without the bedrock
of humility which she strove to practice in every circumstance.
Through consistent prayer, she routed pride and was liberated to
respond to others as she would to Christ.

Asking Therese for her intercession—the help she
promised when she vowed to spend her heaven doing good on
earth—I reflect on how the battle can be won in my own life.

Reflection To prepare myself for the practice of habitual charity, I meditate on the following questions.

In what ways can I, by God's grace, practice "putting up with all my neighbor's faults"?
—By noticing my own faults and the burdens they place on others?
—By following Therese's custom of acting as if my neighbor's faults do not offend me?
—By helping him or her in a humble and nonjudgmental way to overcome these faults?

How can I prepare myself to "never be surprised by his weakness"?
—By reminding myself that, "There, but for you, Lord, go I"?
—By realizing that I have no idea how extensive or how heavy his hidden problems and limitations may be?
—By seeing the plank in my own eye rather than the speck in my neighbor's? (See Mt 7:3.)

How can I manage to be "inspired by the least of his virtues"?
—By seeing him from God's point of view and realizing, as Therese taught, that every good act is pleasing to the Lord?
—By considering the cost to him of this virtuous act?
—By praying for him that he may be moved to greater virtue?

Exploring Further

Response   To internalize the image of the woman warrior, we must
be willing to pray in word and deed as steadily as foot
soldiers facing the daily march. Therese's Little Way leads to a
gradual and unremarked martyrdom. It involves dying to self so
slowly that progress may be invisible to those around us.
Imperceptibly, Christ increases as we decrease.

Begin by memorizing these seven lines of Therese's poem,
"The Eternal Today":

> My life is an instant,
> An hour which passes by;
> My life is a moment
> Which I have no power to stay.
> You know, O my God,
> That to love you here on earth—
> I have only today.

There is a powerful sense of discipline in this simple verse
which, if attended, can help us to overcome the common hurdles
to prayer and charitable action. Try to live one day at a time,
making the most of the opportunities—however small—to
develop selflessness out of love for Jesus. Sufficient to the day are
the skirmishes thereof. Don't wear yourself out rehashing old
battles or fearing future campaigns.

The spirituality of Therese was watered by the Scriptures.
She knew the Word of God and kept it with integrity. Her prayer
life was particularly dependent on the Psalms and the Gospels.
To become better acquainted with the Woman Warrior, pray
these lines from the Psalms over a period of several days:

> For who is God except the LORD?
> Who is a rock, save our God?

> The God who girded me with strength
> > and kept my way unerring;
> Who made my feet swift as those of hinds
> > and set me on the heights;
> Who trained my hands for war
> > and my arms to bend a bow of brass. (Ps 18:32-35)

> Fight, O LORD, against those who fight me;
> > War against those who make war upon me.
> Take up the shield and buckler,
> > and rise up in my defense. (Ps 35:1-2)

Another approach would be to meditate on the Gospel story from which Therese drew her dearest image of Jesus, an image that consoled her during recurrent dry spells of prayer. Reread "The Storm on the Sea" (Mk 4:35-41) several times before reflecting on its message, first to Therese, and then to you.

Can you, like Therese (and unlike the disciples), allow Jesus to sleep in your boat at least occasionally when the waters get rough?

Does your faith require constant reassurance?

Or can you sometimes trust that Jesus is present to you even when he seems to be off in dreamland?

Therese could not have known the following excerpt from a Ute Indian prayer. But it clearly echoes her spirituality. You might record it on a bookmark, a desk blotter or the family bulletin board as your campaign slogan:

> I seek strength,
> not to be superior to my brothers,
> but to be able to fight my greatest enemy—
> myself.

Reading   Follow Therese further along her Little Way in one of these books:

The Autobiography of St. Therese of Lisieux: The Story of A Soul, translated by John Beevers (Garden City: Image, 1957).

Collected Letters, by Therese of Lisieux, translated by F.J. Sheed (New York: Sheed & Ward, 1949).

Prayer and the Present Moment, by Michael Day (Westminster, Maryland: The Newman Press, 1958).

St. Therese of Lisieux: A Spiritual Renascence, by Henri Petitot (London: Burns, Oates & Washbourne, 1927).

Saints for All Seasons, edited by John J. Delaney (Garden City: Doubleday, 1978).

The Search for St. Therese, by Peter-Thomas Rohrbach (Garden City: Hanover House, 1961).

Storm of Glory: The Story of St. Therese of Lisieux, by John Beevers (Garden City: Image Books, 1955).

TERESA
OF AVILA
1515-1582

The Spiritual Mother

Getting to Know Teresa

Life-Sketch Teresa of Avila was a liberated woman who, when the occasion demanded, could put Spanish kings and ponderous prelates in their places. She was an able diplomat who, when her sister Carmelites resented her appointment as their superior, placed a statue of Mary in the prioress' chair, gave her the convent keys and assured the Sisters, "Ladies, here is your prioress." She was a determined reformer who founded a monastery of the primitive Rule at Duruelo and won the affection of an angelic young friar named John of the Cross. Teresa was a woman to be reckoned with.

Born Teresa de Ahumada y Cepeda, one of nine children in a wealthy Spanish family during the Renaissance, she once ran away from home, hauling her reluctant older brother Roderigo with her, to be martyred by the Moors. She counted martyrdom "a bargain price" for getting into heaven. To her, it was a simple matter of common sense: "I want to see God, and to see him we must die." At that early stage in her life, her desire was prompted more by curiosity and a yen for adventure than by devotion.

A strong-willed girl with an artillery of charm, intellect and wit, Teresita filled her head with tales of chivalrous (and illicit) love, and her hours with idle chatter. She was torn between the religious influence of her parents and the vanities of social life among the nobility. After her mother's death when Teresa was 15, she was sent to the convent school of Our Lady of Grace, a measure intended to break up her romantic attachment to a young cousin.

Teresa loved being in love but dreaded what she called "the slavery of marriage." Women were considered decidedly inferior creatures in her day; she often reflected that prejudice in her own remarks about "ignorant," "weak" or "foolish" women.

When she decided, for the safety of her soul, to enter religious life, Teresa chose the Convent of the Incarnation, known for its laxity in observing the Carmelite Rule. There she spent much of her time at the parlor grille, gossiping with wealthy friends (including handsome *hidalgos* whose interest in her was not totally spiritual). She was determined to make a go of her vocation. But, because of her considerable natural gifts, she was her own worst enemy.

The attractive young Carmelite hovered like a hummingbird over scented blossoms that might have poisoned her. She narrowly averted a love affair with a lapsed priest who was fascinated by her beauty and religious aspirations. He left his mistress and was converted, but Teresa, plagued by guilt, became ill to the point of death. Healed through the intercession of St. Joseph, she returned to her destructive habit of wavering between God and the world. The struggle wore on for 20 years until the death of her father, whose holiness led her to a rededication of her religious life.

Even then her conversion was incomplete. Another 10 years slipped away before Teresa could remain faithful to mental prayer. "Up until now it has been my life," she wrote. "Now God lives in me." Unfortunately, her progress was often impeded by half-baked spiritual directors who attributed her visions of Christ to the devil. But Teresa persevered and began to experience the constant presence of Jesus "like a person in a dark room whom you cannot see but you know is there." She grew in mysticism, self-sacrifice and charity, more than making up for lost time.

Realizing that her commitment to prayer could not survive in the scandalous Convent of the Incarnation, Teresa initiated a return to the austere Rule of Carmel. She founded, despite rigorous opposition and scanty resources, the reformed Convent of St. Joseph at Avila in 1562. She was 47 years old and her life was just beginning. Her next two decades would be characterized by adventure and accomplishment beyond anything she had dreamed about as a romantic teenager.

Mother Teresa of Jesus founded 17 convents and one monastery of the primitive Rule. She entrusted the reform of Carmelite men's houses to her friend Fray John of the Cross. Like Ignatius of Loyola, her contemporary, she was an organizing genius whose persuasive force and energetic prayer overcame all obstacles. Her motto was, "To act, to suffer, to love." She lived it with an intensity that made her a recognized saint long before her death at 67.

Shortly before she died, Teresa wrote the following lines of advice on a bookmark. They speak as directly to us as they did to her contemporaries:

> Let nothing disturb you,
> Nothing affright you.
> All things pass,
> God is unchanging.
> Patience obtains all:
> Whoever has God
> Needs nothing else,
> God alone suffices.

Portrait   To know Teresa of Avila is to love her. She is a spiritual mother, a warm, confident, capable person at whose knee we find comfort and wise counsel. Of all the popular saints, no one has given more practical advice for beginners in prayer than the great Teresa. Because of her own decades-long difficulties with prayer, she understands the reluctance and insecurity of those who want to pray regularly but cannot seem to stick with it.

Her compatriots knew Teresa as a talented woman who balanced action and contemplation with consummate grace. The Carmelite habit, although it hid her curly chestnut hair, merely emphasized her high forehead, arched eyebrows and the dimples that announced her playful sense of humor. She paired charm with political savvy, common sense with intellectual mastery, humility with awareness of her own capabilities. Declared a doctor of the Church, she had only two years of formal schooling.

If, instead of traversing 16th-century Spain in a mule cart to establish new convents, she were doing the same in 20th-century America, La Madre Teresa would surely be quoted in

Time. Her *bons mots* make entertaining reading in any age:

> Well, Lord, if this is how you treat your friends, no wonder you have so few!
>
> From silly devotions and sour-faced saints, good Lord, deliver us!
>
> God gives us much to suffer for him, if only from fleas, wicked boys and bad roads!
>
> I won't have nuns who are ninnies!
>
> At prayer time, pray; at partridge time, partridge!
>
> There are no worse robbers than those we carry within ourselves.
>
> If obedience sends you to the kitchen, remember that the Lord walks among the pots and pans and that he will keep you in inward tasks and in outward ones, too.

The profusion of exclamation points underscores Teresa's passionate intensity.

Her advanced spirituality, characterized by mystical prayer and dramatic visions, did not prevent her from enjoying the pleasures of castanets and fancy pastries on feast days. Her immense capacity for life echoes through her correspondence.

The prioress' letters are laced with favorite recipes, herbal cures, administrative and marital tips, diplomatic overtures, jokes, and reprimands to those who had earned them. These letters were often penned in great haste as she juggled her duties as foundress, superior, spiritual director and author. Since there was never time to polish what she had written, she bluntly advised one correspondent, "If I miss out a letter, put it in yourself."

Prayer was the only occupation for which she always had time.

Prayer-Life   In obedience to her confessors, Teresa wrote three books recording her spiritual progress and guiding others in the art of prayer: her *Autobiography*, *The Way of Perfection*, and *The Interior Castle*. The last is her masterpiece. It is based on a vision Teresa had of the soul as a crystal castle with lights radiating from a fire in its midst. Each region of light marks a stage of interiorization, a "mansion" in which a certain level of prayer has been achieved. The King of Glory resides in the center of the soul, the seventh mansion, where profound union with him is attained.

From experience, Teresa was able to describe each stage of the interior passage in vivid detail. Those who are able to follow her to the seventh mansion discover the truth of Jesus' promise:

> "Anybody who loves me
> will be true to my word,
> and my Father will love him;
> and we will come to him
> and make our dwelling place with him." (Jn 14:23)

While the *Castle's* appeal is primarily to those who seek an advanced technique of prayer, Teresa's *Way of Perfection* is a gold mine for beginners. She had the sense to include several chapters on *vocal* prayer, realizing that for many people vocal prayer is the only prayer. Teresa knew that *mental* prayer is as intimidating to some as a private audience with the pope or a debate with William F. Buckley. But if she were writing today, she would be the first to assure us that we do not need a master's degree in theology or a halo to practice mental prayer.

"Mental prayer, in my view, is nothing but friendly intercourse, and frequent solitary converse, with him who we know loves us," she wrote in her *Autobiography*. She advised young Carmelites to recall the companionship of Jesus as often as possible and to be firm in their efforts to remain recollected. Admitting that the work of enclosing our ceaseless thoughts and imaginings within the soul can be tiresome, she observed that the body, by insisting on its rights to rest or diversion, is "cutting off its own head."

Letting Teresa Teach Us

Approach   In her approach to prayer, Teresa shows a level-headedness and psychological insight that readily puts beginners at ease. She starts with vocal prayer—focusing on the familiar ground of the Our Father—and moves imperceptibly, painlessly into mental prayer. The novice is never quite sure when she or he has crossed the line. La Madre makes the transition seem as natural as going from dialogue into devoted silence with a loved one.

She recommends disciplined attention to God our Father "because it is impossible to speak to him and to the world at the same time." She also realizes, however, that this is sometimes easier said than done. Assuring her followers that prayerful concentration can be very difficult during stress or illness or "when our heads are tired," she advises simply praying as best they can or busying themselves with some virtuous action.

Her reasonableness is irresistible. How can we reject a teacher who assures us that there's no point in worrying about our occasional inability to pray? "You musn't weary yourself by trying to put sense into something—namely your mind—which is for the moment without any," she quips.

The beginner should be forewarned that Teresa has a reputation for persuading people to her point of view. Her biographies are rich with examples of those who opposed her will and were won over: her brothers, her community, the unreformed Carmelites, King Philip II and Church authorities. She enlists her considerable eloquence and empathy to win us over to mental prayer, the door to the interior castle.

sideration   Are we willing to be persuaded by Teresa that the Our Father (or any vocal prayer) can lead us into a meaningful experience of mental prayer?

Are we open to her advice that whenever we pray the

Lord's Prayer we imagine Jesus by our side teaching it to us alone?

Invocation La Madre,
teach me to pray
as you once taught the novices at St. Joseph of Avila.
I trust in your seasoned direction.
Because you struggled for 20 years with mental prayer,
you can understand my insecurities and weaknesses,
my habit of procrastinating.
Today, right now,
I am ready to pray.
Do your best with me.
Mother my spiritual progress.
Come, Holy Spirit,
open the door to my interior castle!

Praying With Teresa: St. Joseph's Chapel

Meditation St. Joseph's is your favorite foundation, Teresa, because it was your first convent of the austere primitive Rule. Once a small private home, San Jose was made possible by "God and Teresa and 1,000 donated ducats." You designed the chapel, installing the community's protectors at its doors: the Blessed Mother holding her infant Son and St. Joseph dressed in an embroidered tunic. A high grille separates the interior altar from the exterior chapel where visitors come to Mass.

The altar is adorned only with two candles and a white silk altar cloth. A sanctuary lamp glows above the tabernacle. You are at home here, away from the luxuries of the Convent of the Incarnation. You can live as an enclosed nun, in poverty and penance, moving ever closer to the realization of your childhood dream: "I want to see God, and to see him we must die."

An imposing figure in a brown habit with black veil and white cape, you sit on a bench against the wall. Sister Isabel, a young novice, settles back on her heels so that she can look up at you or to the altar without changing position. She has come to you for the advice you are writing into *The Way of Perfection*.

Before beginning, you lean over, sign the cross on Isabel's forehead and pat her cheek. "Wouldn't it be thought stupid if we didn't know who we were or where we came from?" you ask, prompting a smile from the novice. "Well, then, consider our own ignorance if we, as persons of prayer, make no attempt to discover our real identities and know only that we are dwelling in these bodies."

You explain that, for all of us, self-knowledge must grow hand in hand with prayer. Whenever we pray, in the formal sense of a time set aside for that purpose, we should begin and end with an examination of our conduct, our motivation, our relationship with God. It was by avoiding such analysis that you were able to put off a commitment to prayer for so long. You are determined to help others avoid the same mistake.

"Self-knowledge is the bread which must be eaten with every dish, even the daintiest.... There is no nourishment without that bread," you insist. Isabel nods solemnly. Together you remain silent for several minutes.

After this brief but daily examination of conscience, you counsel, we should reverently make the Sign of the Cross and then look for a companion. "And what better companion could we find than Jesus himself, the very Master of prayer, who never leaves us and from whose side we should never depart?"

Isabel recognizes the leitmotiv of your teaching: the constant presence of Christ and our knowing, believing, remembering that he is there like a friend in a dark room, like a lover who, even when physically absent, is present in our hearts.

You urge Isabel to turn to Jesus and say with the disciples: "Lord, teach us to pray, as John taught his disciples" (Lk 11:1). Then you lead her slowly through the prayer Jesus taught his friends:

Our Father in heaven,
hallowed be your name,
your kingdom come,
your will be done
on earth as it is in heaven.
Give us today our daily bread,
and forgive us the wrong we have done
as we forgive those who wrong us.
Subject us not to the trial
but deliver us from the evil one. (Mt 6:9-13)

From the sleeve of your habit you bring out a picture of Jesus. You study it, like a dark-eyed child content with her most valued possession. Then you give it to Isabel, saying, "You will find it most helpful if you use this icon or any other image of the Lord that you find appealing. Turn to it regularly, whenever you want to talk to him, and he will tell you what to say."

Isabel takes the icon, remembering vaguely the face of a beautiful doll she meditated on as a child. "Shall I not become like a little child again by focusing on this picture of the one I love to learn to pray?" she asks herself.

Feeling insecure, the novice voices her doubts about what to say. You shush her with a wave of your hand. "If words do not fail you when you talk to people on earth, why should they fail you when you talk to God? Do not imagine that they will—I shall certainly not believe that they have done so if you once form the habit."

Isabel knows that further objections are useless. You do not take no for an answer—particularly when it comes to prayer.

All that is required, you insist, is to develop the habits you have already outlined and adhere to them. If Isabel invokes the help of the Holy Spirit and wills herself to pray regularly—even when she thinks it is a total loss—she will soon be rewarded. God will not allow the beginner to go on struggling without encouragement. Soon, you promise, "We shall realize that the bees are coming to the hive and entering it to make honey, and all without any effort of ours."

Reminding Isabel to use her icon as an aid to recollection, you advise her to consider how eager Jesus is to have us understand and profit by the prayer he gave us. "Consider also how senseless vocal prayer is if not accompanied by a realization of who is being addressed and who first offered the prayer. We must develop this realization if we would pray as mature Christians," you observe.

You suggest Isabel find some quiet place to be alone with Jesus, speak a line of Our Father, and then consider its meaning. Right at the start, you explain, Jesus grants us the greatest possible blessing by sharing his Father with us.

Our Father in heaven.

Our Father, Jesus assures us, cannot forget us. He must forgive us as he forgave the Prodigal; he must comfort and sustain us as a true Father is bound to do. Our Father cherishes us, sharing with us his only Son, making us daughters and sons and heirs of his Kingdom. What more could we ask of a loving Father?

With Jesus, we say "Our Father." And who is this Father whom we address so confidently?

"Whoever has seen me has seen the Father....
Do you not believe that I am in the Father
and the Father is in me?
The words I speak are not spoken of myself;
it is the Father who lives in me accomplishing his works."

(Jn 14:9-10)

"Father, that I may be one with you and your Son!"

You pause, Teresa, allowing the chapel to be filled with a stillness emating from the tabernacle. Isabel gazes from the altar to her icon, protecting her recollection from intrusion. "May the Holy Spirit enkindle your will and bind you to himself," you say, continuing the lesson.

Hallowed be your name. Your kingdom come.

Here, you explain, Jesus entreats his Father on our behalf. And what does he ask?

He does not say, "Give us, Father, whatever is good for us." He realizes that we, in our weakness, need to ask for particular things that make us stop and think about what we are requesting. Jesus knows that we cannot hallow (praise, glorify, exalt) our Father's name unless he shares his Kingdom with us here on earth. The two petitions are interdependent.

Jesus wants us to anticipate the joys of heaven, where our only concern will be to love and praise the Father. Now is the time, while we are yet on pilgrimage, to taste these joys in mental prayer. For when our faculties (intellect and imagination) are tranquil and our souls receptive, Jesus gives us a glimpse of the life that will be ours when we come into the fullness of his Kingdom.

At this point, you want to impress on Isabel the nature of the prayer of quiet into which the soul may enter while reflecting on vocal prayer. In this state, the soul is perfectly still. No words or images enter it. Although it does not see God, it knows without doubt that he is near. A feeling of deep satisfaction and delight pervades the soul which hopes that this state will last forever.

Realizing that the novice does not understand, you use an analogy suggested in contemplation. The soul is like a baby at its mother's breast. The baby does not have to cry or even move its lips to receive milk because the mother's love is so great that she gives without being asked. In the prayer of quiet, the soul simply loves and does nothing. No effort is required. The Lord, like a solicitous mother, nourishes it freely without being asked.

Your will be done, on earth as it is in heaven.

Jesus must accomplish in us this promise which he made to his Father in our behalf. Alone, we cannot do the Father's will. But his will, whether we like it or not, must be done. If we cling to our self-will, we make a mockery of these words every time we pray the Our Father.

Only by uniting ourselves with Jesus can we pray, "Your will be done." His is the obedience we seek:

> He withdrew from them about a stone's throw,
> then went down on his knees
> and prayed in these words:
> "Father, if it is your will,
> take this cup from me;
> yet not my will but yours be done." (Lk. 22:41-42)

The Father will answer this prayer for each of us according to our sincerity in desiring his will, our courage to carry it out, the strength of our love for him. To say, "Your will be done," and withdraw the offer as soon as any trial appears is like holding out a jewel to the Lord and, when he reaches to receive it, grabbing it back.

Do we mean what we say, "Your will be done"? Or do we imagine that we are just being polite to the Father or saying what he wants to hear? Are we like the son who said yes to his father's request that he work in the vineyard and then never bothered to do so (see Mt 21:28-32)?

We must consider that the Father's will may mean illness or persecution or dishonor or trials of many kinds which we would not choose for ourselves. Can we say yes to these possibilities? Only if Jesus says yes in us.

Sensing that Isabel has absorbed enough for one session, you bless her again and go to the altar to kneel for a closing examination of conscience. You recall the actions, attitudes and desires that have characterized your day, and look squarely at the areas where your will has conflicted with the Father's. "At this moment, Lord, I see that I am so guilty in your sight that everything I might have to suffer would fall short of my deserts." You resolve that tomorrow you will be more prayerful and, consequently, more virtuous in action.

117

As the two of you leave the chapel, Isabel reveals her persistent feelings of unworthiness in prayer. What will she say to the Lord when you are not there to guide her? What if she is overcome with her own inadequacy? Laughing, you respond, "Avoid being bashful with God, as some people are, in the belief that they are being humble."

If we are too humble to speak honestly to Jesus and allow him to speak to us, we are entirely too humble.

Reflection To avoid helplessness in prayer, Teresa of Avila suggests three basic props:
  —Be content with vocal prayer when mental prayer is too difficult. Vocal prayer in itself brings many blessings.
  —Use spiritual or meditative reading as an aid to recollection.
  —Find an image or an icon of Jesus that helps you to focus on him in prayer.

Am I already faithful to one or more of these practices? If not, when will I begin?

Praying Like Teresa: A Chapel of My Choice

Meditation Jesus,
       you revealed yourself to Teresa in mystical prayer.
       The union she attained I am also bold enough to seek.
       In wisdom, she advises me to imitate the disciples
       who came to ask you how to pray.
       She has set me on the right path.
       Now she leaves me in your hands
       that I may learn to pray the Our Father as though for the
          first time,
       as though, even before the disciples,

you were teaching this prayer to me.
Speak, Lord, I am listening.

Desire therefore my words;
   long for them and you shall be instructed. (Wis 6:11)

In my imagination, I find myself in a solitary chapel
which is designed and furnished as a fitting place for prayer. On
either side of the altar are icons of Our Lady and Teresa of Avila.
On the veil of the tabernacle I see an image of Jesus which will
help me to experience his presence.

As I reflect on the familiar words of the Our Father, Jesus
speaks. I hear him with my interior senses. He instructs me as he
taught Teresa when she prayed for insight into the prayer he
loved above all others. Reining in will, memory and intelligence,
I train my attention on his image and listen for *his* voice as I pray:

"Give us today our daily bread."

*I myself am the bread for which you petition the Father. I am
the Bread of Life every day of your life. My Father has made me a gift
to you, a gift that remains with you until the end of the world. Because
I took your humanity on myself in loving obedience, I am one with you
in making this plea. By the Father's accord, I remain with you as the
bread that encourages and nourishes, satisfies and sustains.*

> *I myself am the living bread*
> *come down from heaven.*
> *If anyone eats this bread*
> *he shall live forever;*
> *the bread I will give*
> *is my flesh, for the life of the world. (Jn 6:51)*

*Do not dwell on the bread that perishes. Fix your desire on
higher things and pray that the Father will give you the capacity to
enjoy them always. I have warned you not to worry about what you
will eat. Have you forgotten my refusal to turn stones into bread after*

40 days of fasting? The only bread I sought was the Word that came from the mouth of my Father. Would I teach you to do less?

When you pray, think only of the bread that gives eternal life. And when you eat this bread, be not blind to my presence. See me entering your house just as I entered the house of Martha and Mary, the house of Zacchaeus the tax collector. Come into your house with me. Sit at my feet like Mary. Or across the table from me, basking in the welcome you see on my face as Zacchaeus did (see Lk 19:1-10). Unbind your faith so that you may see me, whether you feel any devotion or not.

The man or woman who feeds on me will have life because of me. Pray with sincerity that the Father will always give you your daily bread.

"And forgive us the wrongs we have done,
as we forgive those who wrong us."

Have you truly considered the meaning of these words? Do you fear their implication? Do you see what is taken for granted in this request?

In seeking the Father's mercy, you are assuring him that you have already—at least in intention—shown mercy to those who have in any way harmed, insulted or persecuted you. This is the very reason my saints sought out trials and difficulties as ardently as the unenlightened seek wealth and honors. They did not want to approach the Father with empty hands, having nothing to forgive others.

If only you realized how trifling are the wrongs most good people forgive! They count themselves merciful when they forgive even the slightest wrong—or imagined injustice—done against them. My daughter Teresa understood the harm in forgiving slights as though they were grievous insults like those I bore out of love for you. She recognized that such people are like children building houses of straw. When a storm comes, they are blown away. Their false sense of honor weakens them.

When you seek our Father's forgiveness, then, know that you are receiving a gift from one who loves you without measure. Think not of how merciful you have managed to be, but of how much in need of mercy you always are. Realize that you have not merited the forgiveness you seek. Your plea will be answered because you ask in my name.

And exercise your capacity to forgive whenever the opportunity arises. Mutual love is the most difficult virtue—even among those who hope for perfection. Yet it is the virtue most desired by the Father. Reflect often on my parables of forgiveness so that you may learn the nature of mercy. Live on in my love. That is what I expect of you.

> The command I give you is this,
> that you love one another. (Jn 15:17)

Recall the story of the merciless official (see Mt 18:21-35). Although his master took pity on him, he showed no pity to his fellow servants. Because of his hard-heartedness, he was handed over to the torturers. This was my way of telling you that you must forgive others from your heart. If you do not, your prayer is worthless.

"Subject us not to the trial, but deliver us from the evil one."

Do you know why I gave you this petition to offer to the Father, knowing that you will certainly experience, as I did, both trial and temptation?

When you make this petition, you are acknowledging your dependence on God, your absolute need for protection from the evil one who would separate you from the Father. Your need is ever-present, especially when you are least aware of it.

Identifying evil with obvious sinfulness—crime, lust, violence—you leave yourself open to attack by way of false virtue, complacency and untried humility. I opened Teresa's eyes to this danger ("We think we are walking safely, when, without realizing it, we stumble and fall into a pit from which we cannot escape"), and I alert you to it.

The evil one knows you well; his temptations are tailored to your spiritual infirmities. By clouding your mind with worry over past sins, he convinces you that you are unworthy to receive the Eucharist or to serve me in some ministry. When you should be thinking of God's mercy, you are concentrating on your own wretchedness. He would make you give up even prayer by persuading you that I do not hear you.

To sour love within your family or among your friends, he magnifies the faults of others while blinding you to your own shortcomings. He insinuates destructive intentions where there is only forgetfulness or lack of understanding. He amplifies harmless personal habits into intolerable distractions. He brews anger and impatience by stirring up your feelings of insecurity, resentment, possessiveness. He fathers the communication gap between you and others.

Can you withstand these subtle attacks alone? Can you, unaided, avoid falling into the pit?

> *Wake up, and pray*
> *that you may not be subjected to the trial. (Lk 22:46)*

Pray that our Father will deliver you from these and all the snares that lie in wait for those who are not vigilant. Pray that no trial may ever separate you from me. And I pray for you as I prayed for my disciples:

> *"O Father most holy, protect them with your name which you*
> *   have given me*
> *[that they may be one, even as we are one].*
> *I do not ask you to take them out of the world,*
> *but to guard them from the evil one." (Jn 17:11, 15)*

Now stay with me awhile longer without words. I am here in the very center of you. Rest in me as I rest in you.

Reflection   In the Our Father we find "enshrined all contemplation and perfection," Teresa says. In this one prayer, Jesus teaches us the whole process of prayer from a vocal offering to the highest contemplative union. We should never tire of it, never assume that we have fully understood its meaning.

> How can I break the habit of saying the Our Father as mindlessly as I might pass the time of day with a neighbor?

> Do I agree that it is better to pray one Our Father with loving attention than 20 Our Fathers without sincerity?

Exploring Further

Response   As a postscript to the meditation, Teresa reminds us that the physical image of Jesus is an aid to beginners, not a permanent prop for those who wish to grow in mental prayer. With her usual forthrightness she asks, "Wouldn't it be foolish if we had a portrait of someone whom we dearly loved and, when the person himself came to see us, we refused to talk with him and carried on our entire conversation with the portrait?"

If we value Teresa of Avila as a spiritual director, we will approach all vocal prayer (the Our Father, the Hail Mary, the Creed, the Psalms, the liturgy) aware of three basic questions:
1) Who am I talking to?
2) Who is making this prayer?
3) What is the object of this prayer?

Once we have answered these questions, we can begin to pray, knowing that we are truly praying rather than talking absentmindedly to ourselves or to some being too distant to notice that our hearts are not in it. Consider the Lord's warning to the Israelites:

> Since this people draws near with words only
>   and honors me with their lips alone,
>   though their hearts are far from me,
> And their reverence for me has become
>   routine observance of the precepts of men,
> Therefore I will again deal with this people
>   in surprising and wondrous fashion:
> The wisdom of its wise men shall perish
>   and the understanding of its prudent men be hid.
>
>   (Is 29:13-14)

Practice Teresa's three-point program for beginners in serious prayer:
1) Start with attentive vocal prayer.
2) Nourish vocal prayer with spiritual reading.

3) Focus on a Christ icon while praying vocally and
   mentally.

Possible resources for spiritual reading, along with any
contemporary translation of the Bible, include:

Let's Start Praying Again, by Bernard Bassett (Image,
   1972).

Beginning to Pray, by Anthony Bloom (Paulist, 1970).

We Dare to Say Our Father, by Louis Evely (Image, 1975).

The Father Is Very Fond of Me, by Edward J. Farrell
   (Dimension, 1975).

The Courage to Pray, by Karl Rahner and Johann B. Metz
   (Crossroads, 1981).

If you do not already have a Christ icon, you might
consider copies of any of the following diverse works of art:
Rembrandt's "Head of Christ"; Leonardo de Vinci's "Last
Supper"; Titian's "The Savior"; El Greco's "The Savior";
Conegliano's "The Redeemer"; de Rosa's "Jesus Blessing the
Children"; the face from the Shroud of Turin.

Devise a brief method for self-examination to be used
before or after periods of formal prayer. This needn't be a full-
fledged examen digging into the dark corners of the past or a
scrupulous listing of every least failure you might ascribe to
yourself. Make it a mini-survey of daily attitudes, actions and
lapses in your relationship with God. A few pointed questions
will do:

—What negative attitudes about myself and others am I
   harboring?

—Have I been forgiving?

—Have I created closeness rather than distance between
   Jesus and me?

—Have I acted on my good intentions?

—Have I prayed?

To strengthen your facility in moving from vocal into

mental prayer, try reading Scripture passages aloud and then reflecting on what they reveal to you about the Father, the Son or the Spirit. The following passages are in harmony with Teresa's teachings on prayer:

> Acts 17:22-31 ("In him we live and move and have our being.")
> 1 Cor 3:10-17 ("Do you not know that you are the temples of God?")
> Jn 14:23-26 ("We will make our dwelling place with him.")
> Mt 6:5-15 ("This is how you are to pray.")

Finally, take to heart Teresa's commonsense advice. Don't wait until you are perfect—or even until you are converted—but give yourself to prayer today.

Reading   For better acquaintance with Teresa, read one or more of these books:

Autobiography of St. Teresa of Avila, translated and edited by E. Allison Peers (Garden City: Image Books, 1960).

I Want to See God: A Practical Synthesis of Carmelite Spirituality, Vol. I, by Pere Marie-Eugene, O.C.D. (Notre Dame: Fides, 1953).

The Interior Castle, by Teresa of Avila, translated and edited by E. Allison Peers (Garden City: Image, 1961).

La Madre: A Play About St. Teresa of Avila, by Sister Mary Frances (New York: Samuel French, 1959).

Teresa of Avila, by Marcelle Auclair (New York: Pantheon, 1953).

The Way of Perfection, by Teresa of Avila, translated and edited by E. Allison Peers (Garden City: Image, 1964).

JOHN
OF THE CROSS
1542-1591

The Empty Vessel

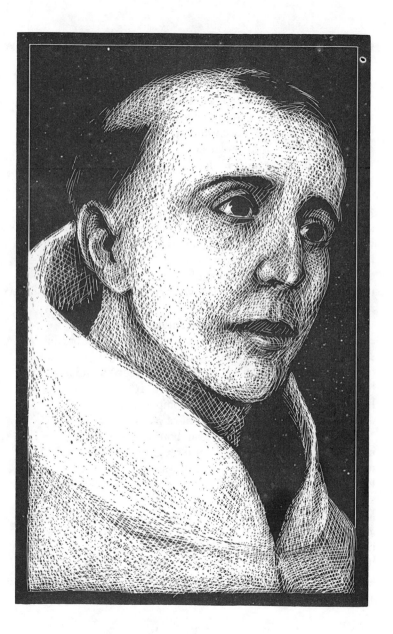

Getting to Know John

Life-Sketch   The life story of John of the Cross has yet to be filmed by a Hollywood producer. Unlike Francis of Assisi, he inspired no legends, no charming vignettes, no romantic biographies. His classics of spirituality have been as appealing to the average reader as the *Politics* of Aristotle. The categories that identify John isolate him behind imposing walls of literary and spiritual superiority.

His books are religious and poetic masterpieces: *The Ascent of Mount Carmel, The Dark Night, The Living Flame of Love* and *The Spiritual Canticle.* They have been praised by critics who were awed by John's poetry and bemused by his mysticism. He may be the only Catholic saint who is better known outside the Church than within. His insight into the human longing for union with the Ultimate is conveyed in a language that entices agnostics and non-Christians.

Because John uses few conventional devotional expressions, his Christian credentials have been questioned by some traditionalists who demand allegiance to familiar religious formulas. The Spanish Carmelite's canonization should long ago have diverted such streams of speculation. It is convenient, however, to criticize a saint whose complexity and originality demand more than a surface reading of pious truisms.

Juan de Yepes y Alvarez was born in Fontiveros, a few miles from Teresa's Avila. His father had been disinherited for marrying a peasant woman and Juan was raised in poverty, learning prayer and compassion for the sick from his mother. As a young man he studied the humanities at the Jesuit College at Medina del Campo and worked in a hospital where he was noted for his solicitude. At the age of 20 he entered the Carmelites, hoping to find the life of contemplation and penance to which his ideals drew him. He continued his advanced studies at the University of Salamanca where he was both student and teacher.

In 1567 Friar John celebrated his first Mass in his

hometown. Here he met Madre Teresa de Jesus, who was about to establish her second foundation of the Carmelite Reform. Teresa of Avila was 52, John 25. Their meeting enkindled an enduring friendship, altered the character of the Order to which they belonged and set the young priest at odds with many of his confreres. When he wanted to go off and join the hermetic Carthusians, Teresa convinced him that he could find all the solitude and austerity he required in the Discalced (barefoot) Carmelites.

No match for her persuasive powers, John agreed to help her turn a small farmhouse at Duruelo into the first men's monastery of the reform movement. There he could indulge his desire for detachment from worldly goods and fast to his heart's content. Duruelo was a training camp, fitting him for the trials to come. He served as confessor to the nuns at Valladolid and later at the reformed Convent of the Incarnation, where he was Madre Teresa's spiritual director. She called him the angelic friar and the father of her soul.

As the Reform (which insisted on democratic elections and a return to the original purity of the Rule) spread to new foundations, John's troubles multiplied. The Calced Carmelites didn't take kindly to the implied criticisms of the reformers. Affronted and perhaps envious, they kidnapped Fray Juan in 1575 and imprisoned him at Medina del Campo. With help from his supporters, he was soon freed by the papal nuncio. His release only stiffened the resolve of his enemies who, a year later, incarcerated him at the priory in Toledo.

John survived in prison on the unlikely diet of sardines, bread and water. He was scourged and humiliated by the friars for his refusal to renounce the Discalced. Suffering repeated abuse that would have broken a lesser man, John turned his solitary hours to prayer and poetry. He composed the poems "The Spiritual Canticle," "The Dark Night of the Soul" and several lesser works before his escape. Astoundingly, he kept the inspired verses in his head since he was not allowed the luxury of writing materials for most of his captivity.

Although he then enjoyed several productive years as a leader of the Reform, a sought-after confessor and writer, John's troubles were not yet over. Later disputes among the Discalced led to his downfall. Ironically, many of the friars wanted to expel him for being too moderate. He was defamed by those who should have lauded him. Deprived of his administrative offices, Juan was still under attack when an infection ended his life at the age of 49.

John of the Cross was remembered by his contemporaries as an empathetic spiritual director who combined unusual psychological insight with intense devotion to Scripture. He knew most of the Bible by heart and, in his maturity, rarely read any other book. Unlike preachers who quote the Bible with heavy-handed gravity, he "spoke of God so delightfully that, when he discoursed upon sacred things at recreation, he would make us all laugh," according to Fray Juan Evangleista.

His spiritual fervor seems to have been as infectious as the chicken pox. Madre Teresa, who loved to tease her young director, commented, "One cannot speak of God to Padre John of the Cross because he at once goes into an ecstasy and causes others to do the same."

Teresa's affection for John is well-documented in her writing. Unfortunately, John's strict insistence on detachment from earthly consolation moved him to burn his accumulated letters from La Madre. We do know that he carried her portrait around with him—an undeniable concession to emotional attachment. Although the two were vastly different in character (she was sometimes irritated by the extremes of his unworldliness), they shared an experience of mystical prayer that bound them as inseparably as avowal to seraphic poverty bound Francis and Clare.

Portrait   "Half a monk" Teresa called him, for John was barely five feet tall and had the insubstantial body of one who fasted as readily as others reach for second helpings. His face was oval with a broad forehead reflecting the breadth of his knowledge;

his eyes had the untroubled look of a wise child. Although he was essentially a contemplative poet, John was loved as well for his willingness to beg alms for the nuns, his readiness to make others laugh despite his own natural seriousness, his good-humored courage in dire circumstances.

Carmelites and lay people who came to him for spiritual counsel treasured the maxims that were a hallmark of his style. A good example is this advice from *The Ascent of Mount Carmel:* "Since the things of the world cannot enter the soul, they are not in themselves an encumbrance or harm to it; rather, it is the will and appetite dwelling within it that causes the damage" (I, 3, 4).

Just as his writing still elicits strong responses, John's angelic character drew both admiration and rancor. Like Francis, he made extreme demands on himself and at times held high expectations of others. The sweetness of his temperament may have riled Teresa when she felt that a bit more ambition or aggressiveness might have helped the progress of the Reform. But above all, John was a spiritual genius who penetrated divine things with laser-like illumination.

His particular appeal to explorers in prayer is his gift for communicating the presence of God through the written word. The language of his poetry holds hidden depth charges that reverberate in the heart of the reader. Even those who understand little of his mystical theology intuit his message: God is real and reachable, loving and lovable. To approach this "living flame of love," we must with Christ die to self and rise again. If we empty ourselves, God will become our fullness.

John conveys the experience of divine union in alluring images of love and desire, darkness and light, annihilation and fulfillment. He sings of *toda y nada* (all and nothing)—God and the nothing that remains after we empty ourselves of desire for anything but him. The poet compels us by the force of sexual imagery to admit the intensity and intimacy of God's personal love for us. Like the singer of the Song of Songs, he urges us to recognize an impassioned God who speaks softly to us:

> "Arise, my beloved, my beautiful one,
> and come!" (Song 2:10)

Those who would follow John through the prose explications of his inspired poetry must be prepared to cast off into deep waters, to float in outer space. Familiar landmarks are few; terra firma always miles away. Much of his work is beyond the province of beginners in spiritual venturing. *The Ascent of Mount Carmel,* however, was written for religious who were just setting out on the climb to perfection. For four centuries it has been consulted by serious students of contemplative prayer.

Popular interest in centering and the Jesus Prayer may clear the way for a rediscovery of *The Ascent.* Although it is only an introduction to John's spirituality, the book guides us toward that detachment which is a prelude to mystical union.

The climb, even in the early stages, is not easy going. Like Everest, Mount Carmel demands respect and discipline. At first the native guide appears to be coolly impersonal, always speaking from a foothold far above us. Unlike Teresa, he reveals none of his personal circumstances along the way. His single aim is to lead us upward by the trail he has mapped out. Gradually, as his voice and eccentric style become familiar, we can warm up to John as one who has our highest good in mind.

The Ascent is a prose commentary on John's poem, "The Dark Night of the Soul."

The introduction and the first few stanzas of that love song give a taste of John's style:

> *A song of the soul's happiness in having passed through the dark night of faith, in nakedness and purgation, to union with its Beloved.*

> 1. One dark night,
> Fired with love's urgent longings
> —Ah, the sheer grace!—
> I went out unseen,
> My house being now all stilled;

> 2. In darkness, and secure,
> By the secret ladder, disguised,

—Ah, the sheer grace!—
In darkness and concealment,
My house being now all stilled;

3. On that glad night,
   In secret, for no one saw me,
   Nor did I look at anything,
   With no other light or guide
   Than the one that burned in my heart,

4. This guided me
   More surely than the light of noon
   To where He waited for me
   —Him I knew so well—
   In a place where no one else appeared.

5. O guiding night!
   O night more lovely than the dawn!
   O night that has united
   The Lover with His beloved,
   Transforming the beloved in her Lover.

ver-Life John's approach to prayer is a gradual, determined and
difficult self-emptying. A soul that is heavy with desires—
for persons, possessions, knowledge, fame—cannot soar.
There is nothing wrong with created beings and things; the
problem lies in our desire for them apart from and in
competition with our love of God. In the first two books of
The Ascent, John describes the obstacles beginners face on
their climb and gives advice about how to overcome them.
Along the way he uses scriptural allusions and images from
everyday life—a gospel approach that gives the uninitiated
reader confidence.

    A favorite image of John's is the strong-willed child. He
compares souls who do not trust to God their progress in
prayer to toddlers who tearfully insist on walking when their
mothers want to carry them, and make no progress toward
their goal.

    When he speaks of desires that run us ragged, he
compares them to restless and discontented children who are

always demanding something from their mothers. While much of John's writing is as intelligible to the beginner as a computer print-out, these homely images communicate with the immediacy of TV commercials.

John, like St. Paul, urges us to put away childish things (see 1 Cor 13:11). He says that when we follow our senses into attachment to the things, persons or situations that stand between us and God, we are clinging to spiritual adolescence. We are like teenagers who never want to move beyond partying and dating to the commitment of marriage.

The Carmelite counselor advises us to uproot negative attachments and toss them out through the open doors of memory, understanding and will. Then, when our souls are closed to distractions, Christ can enter just as he passed through the locked doors of the Upper Room after the Resurrection. Pervaded by his peace, we can be oblivious to all else. "The Dark Night of the Soul" concludes with John's description of this union:

> All things ceased; I went out from myself,
> Leaving my cares
> Forgotten among the lilies.

Letting John Teach Us

Approach   Before the climber attacks Everest, he or she makes
several practice ascents, limbering up for the main event.
The same sane approach applies to John's Mount of Perfection. It
cannot be scaled in a day, or even a length of days. Those who
would follow the Carmelite guide to the summit must accept the
long haul.

    The rest of us—less sure of how we feel about heights—
can go along on a day's trek over the smoother terrain of the
lower elevations. If we discover that climbing becomes addictive,
John of the Cross, the guide extraordinaire, will lead us on to the
peak.

Consideration   Are we challenged or put off by John of the Cross and his
ascent toward contemplation?

Might we find in his advice about detachment a truth we
have been ignoring, a truth that could lead us into a more
satisfying experience of prayer?

Invocation   John, I am ready to join you
as you demonstrate the art of climbing the Mount of
    Perfection.
You who are so at home on the heights,
so invigorated by the rarified air of mysticism,
so adept at contemplative trail-blazing,
take me under your wing.
Convince me of the need to travel light,
to let go,
to brave the darkness.
Help me to break out of my prison of preconceptions
    about contemplation,
daring to go beyond where I have been before.

Praying With John:
The Ascent

Meditation   I see you, John, in imagination's eye, at the base of a
magnificent mountain whose summit parts the clouds.
The mountain is a vision in brilliant green and blue, ascending
into imperial white spires and inscrutable faces. It is a mountain
admired by all but attempted by few. Like Ararat and Tabor, it
speaks of God. It is a sign and a promise: "Learn to be empty of
all things and you will see that I am God" (cf. Ps 46:11).

With gratitude for the promise, you begin your ascent.
On your back is an earthenware vessel of considerable weight. It
slows your pace and impairs the pleasure of climbing. As a
mountaineer might whistle to encourage himself, you repeat a
few lines of the advice you gave to others in *The Ascent of Mount
Carmel:*

> To come to the pleasure you have not
> you must go by a way in which you enjoy not.

You come upon a flowered meadow and pause to rest.
The vessel is already too heavy. Considering its contents, you
slowly pour out your longing for a pleasant and extended solitude
in which to pray, to memorize the Scriptures or to contemplate
the beauty of the Lord.

This desire, good as it is, has become an obstacle to your
union with God. He has shown you through the circumstances of
your life that physical solitude is an unattainable luxury. You
must remain involved in the work of reform and in the spiritual
direction of many who rely on you. From now on, you will be
content to live in community and cultivate interior solitude.

The vessel rides more easily on your shoulders as you
continue scaling the mountain. Whenever fatigue lessens your
resolve, turn back again to your own instructions for ascending
Mount Carmel and repeat them like familiar mantras:

> To arrive at being all
> desire to be nothing.

Again the vessel must be lightened if you would reach the summit. You empty out your desire to be justified, to be recognized, to be allowed to pursue your work without persecution, to be sought after as a person of wisdom and holiness. This time the emptying is painful; but the aftermath is relief.

Before you the high precipices beckon like welcoming angels. The bright sun on the snowy slopes spurs you onward. You follow the way of unknowing and unpossessing, laboring less the higher you go. The rhythm of your own words sets your pace:

> When you turn toward something
> you cease to cast yourself upon the all.
> For to go from all to the all
> you must deny yourself of all in all.

Out of the vessel come all your cares about the Reform, the fruition of your counseling, the success of your teaching, the possibility of another imprisonment by those who call themselves your brothers. You let it all flow out, upturning the vessel to be sure no residue of concern remains. As these dark and anxious desires course down the mountain, freedom intoxicates you.

The words of a familiar Psalm carry you onward and upward without effort or fatigue:

> As the hind longs for the running waters,
>   so my soul longs for you, O God.
> Athirst is my soul for God, the living God.
>   When shall I go and behold the face of God? (Ps 42:2-3)

Light on your feet, you are ready to walk into the clouds that shroud the summit and hide the spring you have come to find. Your spirit gives itself, undivided, to prayer. Your senses are ready to surpass their accustomed roles of perception, imagination and meditation by entering into a passive receptivity. The remaining climb is as easy as falling asleep after a day at the seashore. You are aware only of a pleasant thirst and the certainty of the spring.

I can no longer see you, encompassed by clouds. Surely you are drinking peacefully from the spring of wisdom, love and delight. You are enfolded in the "great forgetfulness" that knows nothing but the presence of the God you compared to "a fountain from which everyone draws as much water as the jug he carries will hold."

You and the vessel are one. Your emptiness has been filled by the All. Because you clung to nothing, you have received everything, "Good measure, pressed down, shaken together, running over..." (Lk 6:38). The mountain has yielded its treasure to you.

Although no one can accurately describe the experience of contemplation, John of the Cross employed his poetic gift to hold this passive prayer before our eyes like a stunning summit waiting to be taken. He assures us that the difference between mental prayer (structured meditations) and contemplation is like the difference between preparing a meal and partaking of it. Who among us would prefer the former to the latter if we realized the possibility open to us?

Reflection   Am I attracted, discouraged or put off by the prospect of preparing myself for contemplative prayer? Why?

As I considered John's process of self-emptying, what thoughts did I have about the contents of my own vessel?

Do I believe that detachment is a necessary prelude to deep prayer? Why or why not?

Praying Like John:
My Ascent

Meditation O my God,
you who dwell in the cloud of unknowing,
draw me out of my carefully-wrought security,
from the protective fictions I weave around myself.
Through the guidance of the mystic-mountaineer,
St. John of the Cross,
lead me to the spring of living waters
where I may drink of your delight.
I will, by your grace,
pour out the murky waters of selfish preoccupations.
Because of your constant love for me,
grant me the virtue of detachment
from all that stands between us.

I see myself at the foot of the Mount of Perfection, as awesome to me as the Matterhorn. Unlike those times in my life when I have walked away from a spiritual challenge or pretended it didn't concern me, this time I am determined to place myself in your hands and say, "Lead me."

I will not be dissuaded by my imperfections or my shortcomings in prayer. As John of the Cross reminds me in *The Ascent of Mount Carmel,* "One rosary is no more influential with God than is another....The prayer he hears is that of the simple and pure heart, which is concerned only about pleasing God and does not bother about the kind of rosary used." I cannot say that contemplation is not the rosary for me until I have opened myself to it.

Would I encamp at the base of a mountain if I were assured that by climbing it I would gain a splendid treasure beyond my imagining? Would I fear ascent to a treasure that could never be taken away from me, the value of which would remain eternally beyond price, the possession of which would

141

ensure my lasting happiness? Lord, let me not be so foolish nor so cowardly!

The earthenware vessel on my back is heavy and awkward, but I am eager to begin. John will be my Sherpa, guiding me expertly up narrow trails and steep ridges. He proceeds without haste, aware of my burden and my timorous faith.

The climb, even in this early stage, is difficult. I am constantly aware of the unnecessary burden self-will has shaped for me. John advises that I rest for awhile and consider my vessel's contents. There, in the dark waters, I see my attachments floating like tangled seaweed at low tide. I see my desires

> to be richer,
> to be younger,
> to be more successful,
> to be sought after,
> to be attractive,
> to be a little better off than my relatives, my neighbors, my enemies.

I recognize these entanglements as obstacles to my contemplative union with you, my God. But shedding them is not an easy matter. They have wrapped themselves around me, clinging like tenacious children who demand allegiance to their immature causes. Under John's steady gaze, I tip the vessel, allowing misdirected desires to flow out upon the ground. My sorrow at seeing them go is short-lived as my guide beckons me onward.

Throughout the climb, whenever the weight of the vessel becomes unbearable, I pause to reflect on the attitudes and habits that prevent me from attaining spiritual maturity. I consider my submerged needs

> to dominate other persons,
> to seek revenge,
> to hoard money or goods,
> to be dishonest,

to ignore family responsibilities.

At times these needs become compulsions that drive me away from you and weaken my efforts to pray. Freely now, I pour them all out in anticipation of the greater good to be gained. My back straightens and vitality courses through my body, impelling me upwards. The music of a Psalm drifts through my consciousness:

> Happy the men whose strength you are!
>> their hearts are set upon the pilgrimage:
> When they pass through the valley of the mastic trees,
>> they make a spring of it;
>> the early rain clothes it with generous growth.
> They go from strength to strength;
>> they shall see the God of gods in Zion. (Ps 84:6-8)

Now that my vessel is more manageable, I am beginning to enjoy the heights. I remember how Jesus loved to go up into the mountains to pray, how he gloried in those encounters with you, his Father, in high places. Recalling that he has challenged me to be as perfect as the Father in whose image I am made, I determine once more to empty this vessel of all that prevents me from reaching the summit. There in the dark dregs I perceive those subtle attitudes that belie many of my best intentions. With John's encouragement, I name them and drain them off, one by one:

> my unwillingness to trust you,
> my discontent with the life you have given me,
> my lack of faithfulness in prayer,
> my reluctance to root out the sinful habit that most
>> binds me,
> my refusal to give you first place in my life.

Swinging the empty vessel, I am as happy as a child who has been rewarded for doing what is right. I am beginning to understand John's way of self-forgetfulness and detachment. Empty of self, I am about to be filled. A single strong desire permeates me like the desert's heat:

> O God, you are my God whom I seek;
> for you my flesh pines and my soul thirsts
> like the earth, parched, lifeless and without water. (Ps 63:2)

John has passed beyond my vision, but I no longer need to rely on him. Led by the sound of the spring, I pass lightly through the veil of clouds to the summit of perfection. I approach the spring, bend to it and drink to my soul's content. I drink peacefully, without effort, without cost.

> "But whoever drinks the water I give him
> will never be thirsty;
> no, the water I give
> shall become a fountain within him,
> leaping up to provide eternal life." (Jn 4:14)

Reflection   How has this meditation on the experience of contemplation differed from my usual approach to prayer?

What does this life-giving water of Jesus mean to me?

Can I recognize myself in the image of the empty vessel?

Does the Mount of Perfection remain a challenge to me?

Exploring Further

Response   The image of the empty vessel exerts a potent attraction
for all who are called to contemplative prayer. Our
deepest instinct is the desire to be filled by God. Even though we
call him happiness or peace or love, the object is the same. We
are ever restless until we rest in him and he in us. The surest way
to find that rest, mystics tell us, is to grow in contemplation. So
how do we begin?

Take this advice John of the Cross offers in *The Ascent of
Mount Carmel* and apply it in a specific way each day for a week:

> To come to the pleasure you have not
> you must go by a way in which you enjoy not.

Evaluate the results. Have you become less attached to things,
persons or situations that divide you from God? Have you
become more prayerful in any sense? Are you willing to extend
the effort, week by week?

Make an honest analysis of the pleasures you seek that do
not strengthen your ability to be a God-centered person. (This
category excludes the valid pleasures of family and community
life, of productive work and innocent play, of enjoying and using
nature in the manner of a good steward.)

If this exercise in detachment proves helpful, experiment
further with any or all of the following lines from *The Ascent of
Mount Carmel*:

> To come to possess all
> desire the possession of nothing.
> To arrive at being all
> desire to be nothing.
> To come to the knowledge of all
> desire the knowledge of nothing. (I, 14, 11)

As a reminder of John's teaching on prayer, you could copy the following summary (or your own version of it) on a card to be kept in your Bible or journal:

God leads us to perfection by beginning with what is most exterior in our nature and working upward to what is most interior. He accomplishes this growth of spirituality in three progressive steps:

— Bringing our *bodily senses* into conformity with our spiritual desires by urging us to absorb what is good from external sources like liturgies, homilies, spiritual discussions. This phase should be accompanied by forms of penance that help us gain control of physical appetites.

— Opening our *hearts* to receive his gifts through spiritual direction, dreams and intuitions of divine things, while taking away our taste for all that is not of God.

— Purifying our *interior senses* of understanding and imagination through active meditation and passive contemplation.

To integrate contemplative prayer into your life-style, set aside 20 minutes or more every day for centering. Sit or lie down in a comfortable position with your back straight and your body at ease. Take two or three deep breaths, inhaling and exhaling slowly and deliberately. Realize that for the next 20 minutes you will do nothing, produce nothing, communicate nothing. (Realize too that it will be rough sledding until you can allow yourself to "waste time" in completely passive prayer that may have no discernible effect.)

Select a simple word that appeals to you as a prayer-leaven—a word like *Jesus, Yahweh, Father, Mother, Spirit, Light, Way, Word, Bread, Lamb, Truth, Faithful, Beloved, Counselor, Dove.* Place yourself in the presence of God and call on him to guide you. Repeat your prayer word to yourself as a means of focusing within. When you are ready, let go of the word and be still. Wait. Be.

If you feel yourself slipping out of the prayer and into distraction, repeat your word in a gentle manner. Then be still again. At the close of your centering time, slowly pray the Our Father as a transition from passivity to active involvement. Try to be faithful to the prayer for at least two weeks before you decide whether this form of contemplation is for you.

For further information and guidance on centering, read *Centering Prayer: Renewing an Ancient Christian Prayer Form,* by Basil Pennington (Doubleday, 1980).

As a means of developing your taste for contemplation, spend ample time in the company of these Scripture readings:

God calls Moses on Sinai...Ex 3:1-6, 12-14
The goodness of God...Ps 36:5-9
Yahweh as passionate Lover...Song 1-8
Yahweh and his beloved...Hos 2:8-25
Martha and Mary...Lk 10:38-42
The Samaritan woman...Jn 4:1-26

Reading   Drink a little deeper of John's spirituality in one of these books:

Ascent of Mount Carmel, by John of the Cross, translated and edited by E. Allison Peers (Garden City: Image, 1958).

The Collected Works, by John of the Cross, translated by Kieran Kavanaugh, O.C.D., and Otilio Rodriguez, O.C.D. (Washington: ICS Publishing, 1973).

The Fire and the Cloud: An Anthology of Catholic Spirituality, edited by David A. Fleming (New York: Paulist, 1978).

St. John of the Cross: His Life and Poetry, by Gerald Brenan (Cambridge: Cambridge University Press, 1973).

Saints and Ourselves, edited by Philip Caramon (Garden City: Image, 1958).

Conclusion

nnections In getting to know these ancestor-saints, we have sensed their relationships with each other as well as the connections between their approaches to prayer. We have discovered their unity of purpose and appreciated their diversity of expression which reassures us as we make our way into deeper prayer than we have known before.

Francis and Clare are spirit-mates, Brother Sun and Sister Moon, active and contemplative, wounded herald and anchored soul. Both find their most profound experience of God in meditation on Jesus crucified. Their lives mirror his in praise and suffering.

Francis and Ignatius are brothers in their adventuring souls, vainglorious soldiers cast by Christ as knights of the Kingdom. Both underwent dramatic conversion; both were astoundingly successful as hero-founders of religious orders still on the front lines of the Church. Both are sensual Christians who see creation illuminated by God; they are sensitive to his presence in the flower or the stone, mystic voyagers of inner space.

Therese is linked to Francis and Ignatius by her military self-image and by her missionary zeal. Like Clare she embraced the world from her cloister, where interior warfare became her daily profession. Now she "spends her heaven doing good on earth."

Her Little Way binds her to John of the Cross whose teaching on detachment from selfish desires provided her with a military strategy. Like him, she sought to be an empty vessel from which the bitter waters of egoism had been drained. Both sought to be lost in God as completely as a drop of water in a chalice of wine.

Between John and Teresa of Avila is the bond of mutual spiritual guidance. He was her confessor and director; she was his mother and friend. Hers was the vivid mysticism of the Interior

Castle; his the dark and difficult mysticism of Mount Carmel. She leads us by the familiar way of the Christ icon; he by the steep path and the heavy vessel.

All six share the zeal of reformers. Each called others to a gospel-focused life that would enrich the Church for centuries. They call us now to a reform of our half-hearted prayer lives. They challenge us by their witness, encourage us with their words of advice. They urge us to stop wasting time in the bottomlands of spiritual procrastination. We must head for the high ground.

Can we translate their experience into a meaningful direction for our own prayer lives? Can we allow ourselves to believe in their desire to help us? Or shall we set them back on their pedestals, pretending that is, after all, where saints belong?

Not if Teresa has her way. As she says: "God deliver us from saying, 'Well, I'm no saint.' We must have holy boldness, for God helps the strong, being no respecter of persons, and he will give courage to you and to me."

Celebration   To stir up "holy boldness" and celebrate your progress in prayer, you might want to gather some friends together for a paraliturgy which reflects the advice of the saints we have consulted. Adapt the following suggestions to your own situation and insights.

Opening Song: "Lose Yourself in Me" (Carey Landry, North American Liturgy Resources)

> God, our God,
> we have come into your presence
> with gratitude for your saints
> and with hope that we may be guided
> by their experience of prayer.
> Send your Spirit
> to conceive a new prayer in our hearts,
> a prayer that will grow

and mature
and ripen into union with you.
We ask you this,
together with our brother-beloved, Jesus Christ,
your Son, our Lord. Amen.

First Reading: Phil 2:5-11, Imitating Christ's humility

Silent Reflection

Response: "Canticle of Brother Sun" (See Chapter 1, page 8. If possible, accompany the prayer with nature slides and instrumental music.)

Silent Reflection

Gospel Reading: Lk 22:7-20, The Last Supper (Or choose any Gospel text that lends itself to application of the senses.)

Gospel Meditation: Follow the Ignatian meditation in Chapter 3, pages 65-72.

Silent Reflection

> Lord, we pray that we, like Francis, may bear your image in our bodies, your song of praise in our hearts.
>
>> For this we pray: Jesus, hear us.
>
> Lord, we pray that we, like Clare, may anchor our souls in solitary places where you can be the meaning of our hours.
>
>> For this we pray: Jesus, inspire us.
>
> Lord, we pray that we, like Ignatius, may sense your living presence in the Gospels and experience your vital presence in the liturgy.

For this we pray: Jesus, touch us.

Lord, we pray that we, like Therese, may be fearless warriors turning the sword of the Spirit against our interior enemies.

For this we pray: Jesus, arm us.

Lord, we pray that we, like Teresa, may always pray with certainty that you are beside us, before us, within us, pleading our cause with the Father.

For this we pray: Jesus, pray in us.

Lord, we pray that we, like John of the Cross, may empty ourselves of all desires that do not converge on you.

For this we pray: Jesus, fill us.

Place a Christ icon where all can see it as a reminder that Jesus teaches us how to pray. Then sing or say the Our Father in an unhurried manner.

Silent Reflection

Closing Song: "Take, Lord, Receive" (John Foley, S.J., North American Liturgy Resources)

For alternative celebrations, scan each chapter and select from the Scripture readings suggested under "Exploring Further," as well as from the prayers of Francis, Clare, Ignatius, Therese, Teresa and John of the Cross.

Additional songs to consider are: "Make Me a Channel of Your Peace" by Sebastian Temple; "If I Be Lifted Up" by Gregory Norbet; "Song of Jesus Christ" by Carey Landry; "Dwelling Place" by John Foley, S.J.